The Complete Crock Pot Cookbook

for Beginners

2000+ Days of Easy and Flavorful Slow Cooker Recipes for Effortless Home-Cooked Meals, from Breakfast to Desserts, Snacks, Lunch and Dinner

Terry Stover

Table of Contents

INTRODUCTION

Welcome to the World of Crock Pot Cooking

Imagine coming home after a long, busy day to the inviting aroma of a delicious, homemade meal simmering away, ready to be served. That's the magic of crock pot cooking. In today's fast-paced world, finding the time to cook healthy and satisfying meals can be a challenge. Between juggling work, family, and personal commitments, many of us struggle to put a wholesome dinner on the table. That's where the humble crock pot comes to the rescue — a kitchen tool that not only saves time but also makes cooking accessible and fun for everyone.

This cookbook is designed to guide you through the wonders of slow cooking, a technique that has been a staple in kitchens for generations. Whether you're a seasoned home cook or a complete beginner, this book will show you how to make the most of your crock pot, helping you prepare delicious meals with minimal effort and maximum flavor. From hearty stews and soups to tender roasts and comforting casseroles, this cookbook has something for everyone.

Why Choose Crock Pot Cooking?

The beauty of crock pot cooking lies in its simplicity. With just a few basic ingredients, a bit of preparation, and the push of a button, you can create mouthwatering dishes that taste like they've been cooking all day — because they have! The slow cooking process allows flavors to meld together in a way that stovetop or oven cooking simply can't replicate. This method is perfect for creating rich, flavorful meals that are tender, juicy, and bursting with taste.

Using a crock pot also means less time spent in the kitchen. You can set it and forget it, leaving your crock pot to work its magic while you focus on other tasks. Whether you're at work, running errands, or simply relaxing, you can trust that a delicious meal will be ready when you are. This makes crock pot cooking ideal for busy families, professionals, students, or anyone who wants to enjoy home-cooked meals without the hassle.

Healthy, Wholesome, and Economical Meals

One of the greatest benefits of using a crock pot is the ability to cook nutritious meals without breaking the bank. Slow cooking allows you to use more affordable cuts of meat, like chuck roast or chicken thighs, and transform them into tender, flavorful dishes. The low and slow cooking method breaks down tougher cuts of meat, making them juicy and soft, while still retaining all their natural nutrients.

Additionally, the crock pot is perfect for cooking with fresh vegetables, grains, and legumes, allowing you to create balanced meals packed with fiber, protein, and essential vitamins. Unlike some fast-cooking methods that can strip food of its nutritional value, slow cooking preserves the nutrients, ensuring that every bite is as healthy as it is delicious.

In this cookbook, you'll find recipes that prioritize wholesome ingredients, offering a range of options for various dietary needs — from gluten-free and low-carb to vegetarian and vegan dishes. No matter your preferences, you can enjoy a diverse array of meals that are good for both the body and soul.

Get Creative with Your Crock Pot

Crock pot cooking is incredibly versatile. While many people associate it with traditional comfort foods like chili or pot roast, the possibilities are truly endless. This cookbook will inspire you to think outside the box and get creative with your crock pot. From international flavors like Mexican enchiladas and Thai curries to breakfast favorites like overnight oats and frittatas, you'll discover new and exciting ways to use your crock pot for every meal of the day.

You'll also learn how to adapt and customize recipes to suit your taste preferences or dietary restrictions. Whether you want to add more spice, swap out an ingredient, or adjust cooking times, crock pot recipes are easily modifiable. This flexibility means you can experiment with different flavors, ingredients, and textures, making every meal a unique culinary adventure.

Tips for Successful Crock Pot Cooking

To help you get the most out of your crock pot, this cookbook also includes practical tips and tricks. You'll learn how to choose the right size and type of crock pot for your needs, how to layer ingredients for even cooking, and how to avoid common pitfalls like overcooking or under-seasoning. You'll also find guidance on meal prepping, storage, and reheating, so you can make the most of leftovers and minimize waste.

We'll walk you through some of the basics, such as the importance of browning meat before slow cooking to enhance flavor, or why adding dairy towards the end of the cooking process can prevent curdling. With these handy tips, even the most inexperienced cook can achieve delicious results every time.

Your Crock Pot Journey Starts Here

Whether you're cooking for a family dinner, hosting a casual gathering with friends, or simply preparing meals for the week ahead, this "Crock Pot Cookbook" is here to help you create memorable dishes with ease. Each recipe is crafted with simplicity in mind, using ingredients that are easy to find and techniques that anyone can master.

So, dust off that crock pot sitting in your cupboard or invest in one if you haven't already. It's time to dive into a world of delicious possibilities, where every meal is a chance to create something wonderful, comforting, and nourishing. Let's start slow cooking and enjoy the journey of flavors and aromas that await.

Welcome to the "Crock Pot Cookbook" — where simplicity meets satisfaction, one meal at a time. Happy cooking!

Chapter ①
Breakfasts

Croque Monsieur Strata

Prep time: 10 minutes | Cook time: 4½ hours | Serves 8

- 8 large eggs
- 2 cups whole or low-fat milk
- 6 shakes Tabasco sauce
- 1 tablespoon Dijon mustard
- 8 cups torn soft-crusted French bread (if the crust is crispy, remove it and use
- the center of the bread)
- 8 ounces (227 g) sliced Black Forest ham, cut into matchsticks
- 3 cups shredded Gruyère cheese
- 4 tablespoons (½ stick) unsalted butter, melted

1. Coat the insert of a 5- to 7-quart crock pot with nonstick cooking spray or line the insert with a crock pot liner according the manufacturer's directions. 2. Whisk together the eggs, milk, Tabasco, and mustard in a large bowl until blended. Add the bread and ham to the bowl and stir to saturate the bread and distribute the ham. 3. Spoon half the bread mixture into the crock pot and sprinkle with half the cheese. Repeat the layers and drizzle with the melted butter. 4. Cover and cook on low for 4 hours, until the strata is cooked through (170ºF / 77ºC on an instant-read thermometer). Remove the lid and cook for an additional 30 minutes. 5. Serve the strata from the cooker set on warm.

Breakfast Hominy

Prep time: 5 minutes | Cook time: 8 hours | Serves 5

- 1 cup dry cracked hominy
- 1 teaspoon salt
- Black pepper (optional)
- 3 cups water
- 2 tablespoons butter

1. Stir all ingredients together in a greased crock pot. 2. Cover and cook on low 8 hours, or overnight. 3. Serve warm for breakfast.

Dill-Asparagus Bake

Prep time: 10 minutes | Cook time: 4 to 5 hours | Serves 8

- 1 tablespoon extra-virgin olive oil
- 10 eggs
- ¾ cup coconut milk
- ½ teaspoon salt
- ¼ teaspoon freshly ground black pepper
- 2 teaspoons chopped fresh dill
- 2 cups chopped asparagus spears
- 1 cup chopped cooked bacon

1. Lightly grease the insert of the crock pot with the olive oil. 2. In a medium bowl, whisk together the eggs, coconut milk, salt, pepper, and dill. Stir in the asparagus and bacon. Pour the mixture into the crock pot. 3. Cover and cook on low for 4 to 5

hours. 4. Serve warm.

Overnight Oatmeal

Prep time: 5 minutes | Cook time: 3 to 10 hours | Serves 8

- 3¾ cups old-fashioned rolled oats
- 8 cups water
- ½ teaspoon salt
- 4 tablespoons (½ stick) unsalted butter, cut into
- small pieces
- 2 cups milk or cream, warmed, for serving
- ¼ cup cinnamon sugar for serving

1. Coat the insert of a 5- to 7-quart crock pot with nonstick cooking spray or line the insert with a crock pot liner according to manufacturer's directions. 2. Combine the oatmeal, water, and salt in the cooker. Cover and cook on low for 8 to 10 hours or on high for 3 to 4 hours, until the oats are creamy. Stir in the butter. Serve with warmed milk and cinnamon sugar.

Cornmeal Mush

Prep time: 10 minutes | Cook time: 4 to 6 hours | Serves 15 to 18

- 2 cups cornmeal
- 2 teaspoons salt
- 2 cups cold water
- 6 cups hot water

1. Combine cornmeal, salt, and cold water. 2. Stir in hot water. Pour into greased crock pot. 3. Cover. Cook on high 1 hour, then stir again and cook on low 3 to 4 hours or cook on low 5 to 6 hours, stirring once every hour during the first 2 hours. 4. Serve hot.

Huevos Rancheros

Prep time: 10 minutes | Cook time: 3 hours | Serves 8

- 1 tablespoon extra-virgin olive oil
- 10 eggs
- 1 cup heavy (whipping) cream
- 1 cup shredded Monterey Jack cheese, divided
- 1 cup prepared or homemade salsa
- 1 scallion, green and white parts, chopped
- 1 jalapeño pepper, chopped
- ½ teaspoon chili powder
- ½ teaspoon salt
- 1 avocado, chopped, for garnish
- 1 tablespoon chopped cilantro, for garnish

1. Lightly grease the insert of the crock pot with the olive oil. 2. In a large bowl, whisk together the eggs, heavy cream, ½ cup of the cheese, salsa, scallion, jalapeño, chili powder, and salt. Pour the mixture into the insert and sprinkle the top with the remaining ½ cup of cheese. 3. Cover and cook until the eggs are firm, about 3 hours on low. 4. Let the eggs cool slightly, then cut into wedges and serve garnished with avocado and cilantro.

Nutty Oatmeal

Prep time: 10 minutes | Cook time: 7 hours | Makes 7 cups

- 1 cup chopped walnuts
- Nonstick cooking spray
- 2 cups rolled oats (not instant or quick cooking)
- 1 cup raisins
- 3 cups almond milk
- 1½ cups apple juice
- ⅓ cup honey
- ⅓ cup brown sugar
- ½ teaspoon ground cinnamon
- ¼ teaspoon ground nutmeg
- ¼ teaspoon salt

1. In a small saucepan over medium-low heat, toast the walnuts until fragrant, about 2 minutes, stirring frequently. 2. Spray the crock pot with the nonstick cooking spray. 3. In the crock pot, combine the walnuts, oats, and raisins. 4. In a large bowl, beat the almond milk, apple juice, honey, brown sugar, cinnamon, nutmeg, and salt. Pour the mixture into the crock pot. 5. Cover and cook on low for 7 hours, or until the oatmeal is thickened and tender, and serve.

Nutty "Oatmeal"

Prep time: 10 minutes | Cook time: 8 hours | Serves 6

- 1 tablespoon coconut oil
- 1 cup coconut milk
- 1 cup unsweetened shredded coconut
- ½ cup chopped pecans
- ½ cup sliced almonds
- ¼ cup granulated erythritol
- 1 avocado, diced
- 2 ounces (57 g) protein powder
- 1 teaspoon ground cinnamon
- ¼ teaspoon ground nutmeg
- ½ cup blueberries, for garnish

1. Lightly grease the insert of a slower cooker with the coconut oil. 2. Place the coconut milk, shredded coconut, pecans, almonds, erythritol, avocado, protein powder, cinnamon, and nutmeg in the crock pot. 3. Cover and cook on low for 8 hours. 4. Stir the mixture to create the desired texture. 5. Serve topped with the blueberries.

Sausage Breakfast Risotto

Prep time: 20 minutes | Cook time: 7 hours | Serves 2

- 8 ounces (227 g) pork sausage
- 1 onion, chopped
- 2 garlic cloves, minced
- Nonstick cooking spray
- 1 cup sliced cremini mushrooms
- 1 cup Arborio rice
- 3 cups chicken stock
- ½ cup milk
- ½ teaspoon salt
- ½ teaspoon dried marjoram leaves
- ⅛ teaspoon freshly ground black pepper
- ⅓ cup grated Parmesan cheese
- 1 tablespoon butter

1. In a medium saucepan over medium heat, cook the sausage, onion, and garlic until the sausage is browned, about 10 minutes, stirring to break up the meat. Drain well. 2. Spray the crock pot with the nonstick cooking spray. 3. In the crock pot, combine the sausage mixture, mushrooms, and rice. Add the stock, milk, salt, marjoram, and pepper, and stir. 4. Cover and cook on low for 7 hours. 5. Stir in the cheese and butter. Let stand for 5 minutes, and then serve.

Keto Granola

Prep time: 10 minutes | Cook time: 3 to 4 hours | Serves 16

- ½ cup coconut oil, melted
- 2 teaspoons pure vanilla extract
- 1 teaspoon maple extract
- 1 cup chopped pecans
- 1 cup sunflower seeds
- 1 cup unsweetened shredded coconut
- ½ cup hazelnuts
- ½ cup slivered almonds
- ¼ cup granulated erythritol
- ½ teaspoon cinnamon
- ¼ teaspoon ground nutmeg
- ¼ teaspoon salt

1. Lightly grease the insert of the crock pot with 1 tablespoon of the coconut oil. 2. In a large bowl, whisk together the remaining coconut oil, vanilla, and maple extract. Add the pecans, sunflower seeds, coconut, hazelnuts, almonds, erythritol, cinnamon, nutmeg, and salt. Toss to coat the nuts and seeds. 3. Transfer the mixture to the insert. 4. Cover and cook on low for 3 to 4 hours, until the granola is crispy. 5. Transfer the granola to a baking sheet covered in parchment or foil to cool. 6. Store in a sealed container in the refrigerator for up to 2 weeks.

Breakfast Sausage

Prep time: 10 minutes | Cook time: 3 hours | Serves 8

- 1 tablespoon extra-virgin olive oil
- 2 pounds (907 g) ground pork
- 2 eggs
- 1 sweet onion, chopped
- ½ cup almond flour
- 2 teaspoons minced garlic
- 2 teaspoons dried oregano
- 1 teaspoon dried thyme
- 1 teaspoon fennel seeds
- 1 teaspoon freshly ground black pepper
- ½ teaspoon salt

1. Lightly grease the insert of the crock pot with the olive oil. 2. In a large bowl, stir together the pork, eggs, onion, almond flour, garlic, oregano, thyme, fennel seeds, pepper, and salt until well mixed. 3. Transfer the meat mixture to the crock pot's insert and shape it into a loaf, leaving about ½ inch between the sides and meat. 4. Cover, and if your crock pot has a temperature probe, insert it. 5. Cook on low until it reaches an internal temperature of 150°F (66°C), about 3 hours. 6. Slice in any way you prefer and serve.

Three-Cheese Vegetable Strata

Prep time: 20 minutes | Cook time: 6 hours | Serves 2

- 1 tablespoon extra-virgin olive oil
- 1 tablespoon butter
- 1 onion, chopped
- 2 garlic cloves, minced
- 1½ cups baby spinach leaves
- 1 red bell pepper, chopped
- 1 large tomato, seeded and chopped
- 1 cup cubed ham
- Nonstick cooking spray
- 5 eggs, beaten
- 1 cup milk
- ½ teaspoon salt
- ½ teaspoon dried thyme leaves
- ⅛ teaspoon freshly ground black pepper
- 6 slices French bread, cubed
- 1 cup shredded Cheddar cheese
- ½ cup shredded Swiss cheese
- ¼ cup grated Parmesan cheese

1. In a medium saucepan over medium heat, heat the olive oil and butter. Add the onion and garlic, and sauté, stirring, until tender, about 6 minutes. 2. Add the spinach and cook until wilted, about 5 minutes. Remove from the heat and add the bell pepper, tomato, and ham. 3. Line the crock pot with heavy-duty foil and spray with the nonstick cooking spray. 4. In a medium bowl, beat the eggs, milk, salt, thyme, and black pepper well. 5. In the crock pot, layer half of the French bread. Top with half of the vegetable and ham mixture, and sprinkle with half of the Cheddar and Swiss cheeses. Repeat the layers. 6. Pour the egg mixture over everything, and sprinkle with the Parmesan cheese. 7. Cover and cook on low for 6 hours, or until the temperature registers 160°F (71°C) on a food thermometer and the mixture is set. 8. Using the foil sling, remove from the crock pot, and serve.

Chocolate-Cherry–Stuffed French Toast

Prep time: 15 minutes | Cook time: 6 hours | Serves 2

- Nonstick cooking spray
- 8 slices French bread
- ¾ cup mascarpone cheese
- ½ cup cherry preserves
- ¾ cup semisweet chocolate chips, melted
- 1 cup sliced pitted fresh cherries
- 5 eggs, beaten
- 1 cup milk
- 1 teaspoon vanilla
- ½ teaspoon ground cinnamon
- ¼ teaspoon salt

1. Line the crock pot with heavy-duty foil, and spray with the nonstick cooking spray. 2. Spread one side of each slice of bread with the mascarpone cheese and the cherry preserves. Drizzle with the melted chocolate. 3. Cut the bread slices in half and layer them in the crock pot with the fresh cherries. 4. In a medium bowl, beat the eggs, milk, vanilla, cinnamon, and salt. Pour the egg mixture into the crock pot. 5. Cover and cook on low for 6 hours, or until the mixture is set and registers 160°F (71°C) on a food thermometer. Remove from the crock pot using the foil, slice, and serve.

Egg–Potato Bake

Prep time: 20 minutes | Cook time: 6 hours | Serves 2

- 2 slices bacon, chopped
- 1 cup pork sausage
- 1 onion, chopped
- 1 cup sliced button mushrooms
- 2 garlic cloves, minced
- 1 orange bell pepper, chopped
- Nonstick cooking spray
- 3 russet potatoes, peeled and sliced
- 1 cup shredded Havarti cheese
- ½ cup shredded Colby cheese
- 5 eggs, beaten
- 1 cup milk
- ½ teaspoon salt
- ½ teaspoon dried thyme leaves
- ⅛ teaspoon freshly ground black pepper

1. In a medium skillet over medium heat, cook the bacon and sausage until the bacon is crisp and the sausage is browned, 10 minutes or so, stirring frequently. Remove the bacon and sausage to a paper towel–lined plate to drain. Remove and discard all but 1 tablespoon of drippings from the pan. 2. In the same skillet over medium heat, cook the onion, mushrooms, and garlic in the remaining drippings until tender, about 5 minutes. Remove from the heat and add the bell pepper, bacon, and sausage. 3. Line the crock pot with heavy-duty foil and spray with the nonstick cooking spray. 4. In the crock pot, layer the potatoes, bacon mixture, and cheeses. 5. In a medium bowl, beat the eggs, milk, salt, thyme, and pepper. Pour the egg mixture into the crock pot. 6. Cover and cook on low for 6 hours, or until the temperature reaches 160°F (71°C) on a food thermometer. 7. Using the foil, remove from the crock pot, cut into squares, and serve.

Overnight Apple Oatmeal

Prep time: 10 minutes | Cook time: 6 to 8 hours | Serves 4

- 2 cups skim or 2% milk
- 2 tablespoons honey, or ¼ cup brown sugar
- 1 tablespoon margarine
- ¼ teaspoon salt
- ½ teaspoon ground cinnamon
- 1 cup dry rolled oats
- 1 cup apples, chopped
- ½ cup raisins (optional)
- ¼ cup walnuts, chopped
- ½ cup fat-free half-and-half

1. Spray inside of crock pot with nonfat cooking spray. 2. In a mixing bowl, combine all ingredients except half-and-half. Pour into cooker. 3. Cover and cook on low overnight, ideally 6 to 8 hours. The oatmeal is ready to eat in the morning. 4. Stir in the half-and-half just before serving.

Crustless Wild Mushroom–Kale Quiche

Prep time: 10 minutes | Cook time: 5 to 6 hours | Serves 8

- 1 tablespoon extra-virgin olive oil
- 12 eggs
- 1 cup heavy (whipping) cream
- 1 tablespoon chopped fresh thyme
- 1 tablespoon chopped fresh chives
- ¼ teaspoon freshly ground black pepper
- ⅛ teaspoon salt
- 2 cups coarsely chopped wild mushrooms (shiitake, portobello, oyster, enoki)
- 1 cup chopped kale
- 1 cup shredded Swiss cheese

1. Lightly grease the insert of the crock pot with the olive oil. 2. In a medium bowl, whisk together the eggs, heavy cream, thyme, chives, pepper, and salt. Stir in the mushrooms and kale. Pour the mixture into the crock pot and top with the cheese. 3. Cover and cook on low 5 to 6 hours. 4. Serve warm.

Pumpkin-Pecan N'Oatmeal

Prep time: 10 minutes | Cook time: 8 hours | Serves 4

- 1 tablespoon coconut oil
- 3 cups cubed pumpkin, cut into 1-inch chunks
- 2 cups coconut milk
- ½ cup ground pecans
- 1 ounce (28 g) plain protein powder
- 2 tablespoons granulated erythritol
- 1 teaspoon maple extract
- ½ teaspoon ground nutmeg
- ¼ teaspoon ground cinnamon
- Pinch ground allspice

1. Lightly grease the insert of a slower cooker with the coconut oil. 2. Place the pumpkin, coconut milk, pecans, protein powder, erythritol, maple extract, nutmeg, cinnamon, and allspice in the insert. 3. Cover and cook on low for 8 hours. 4. Stir the mixture or use a potato masher to create your preferred texture, and serve.

Spanakopita Frittata

Prep time: 10 minutes | Cook time: 5 to 6 hours | Serves 8

- 1 tablespoon extra-virgin olive oil
- 12 eggs
- 1 cup heavy (whipping) cream
- 2 teaspoons minced garlic
- 2 cups chopped spinach
- ½ cup feta cheese
- Cherry tomatoes, halved, for garnish (optional)
- Yogurt, for garnish (optional)
- Parsley, for garnish (optional)

1. Lightly grease the insert of the crock pot with the olive oil. 2. In a medium bowl, whisk together the eggs, heavy cream, garlic, spinach, and feta. Pour the mixture into the crock pot. 3. Cover and cook on low 5 to 6 hours. 4. Serve topped with the tomatoes, a dollop of yogurt, and parsley, if desired.

Salmon and Dill Strata

Prep time: 20 minutes | Cook time: 4½ hours | Serves 6 to 8

- 6 large eggs
- 1 cup whole or low-fat milk
- 1 cup sour cream (low fat is okay), plus additional for serving
- 3 cups cooked salmon in chunks
- ¼ cup chopped fresh dill
- ¼ cup finely chopped red onion
- 2 teaspoons grated lemon zest
- ½ teaspoon freshly ground white pepper
- 6 plain or egg bagels, cut into ½-inch pieces
- 1 (8-ounce / 227-g) package cream cheese, cut into ½-inch cubes
- ½ cup drained and chopped capers for serving
- Lemon wedges for serving

1. Coat the insert of a 5- to 7-quart crock pot with nonstick cooking spray or line the insert with a crock pot liner according the manufacturer's directions. 2. Whisk together the eggs, milk, and sour cream in a large mixing bowl until smooth. Fold in the salmon, dill, onion, lemon zest, and pepper. Add the bagel pieces and mix, saturating the bread. 3. Transfer half the mixture to the crock pot and dot with half the cream cheese cubes. Repeat the layers. Cover and cook on low for 4 hours, until the strata is cooked through (170ºF / 77ºC on an instant-read thermometer). Remove the lid and cook for an additional 30 minutes. 4. Serve the strata from the cooker set on warm with the additional sour cream, capers, and the lemon wedges on the side.

Vegetable Omelet

Prep time: 15 minutes | Cook time: 4 to 5 hours | Serves 8

- 1 tablespoon extra-virgin olive oil
- 10 eggs
- ½ cup heavy (whipping) cream
- 1 teaspoon minced garlic
- ¼ teaspoon salt
- ⅛ teaspoon freshly ground black pepper
- ½ cup chopped cauliflower
- ½ cup chopped broccoli
- 1 red bell pepper, chopped
- 1 scallion, white and green parts, chopped
- 4 ounces (113 g) goat cheese, crumbled
- 2 tablespoons chopped parsley, for garnish

1. Lightly grease the insert of the crock pot with the olive oil. 2. In a medium bowl, whisk together the eggs, heavy cream, garlic, salt, and pepper. Stir in the cauliflower, broccoli, red bell pepper, and scallion. Pour the mixture into the crock pot. Sprinkle the top with goat cheese. 3. Cover and cook on low for 4 to 5 hours. 4. Serve topped with the parsley.

Polenta

Prep time: 10 minutes | Cook time:2 to 9 hours | Serves 8 to 10

- 4 tablespoons melted butter, divided
- ¼ teaspoon paprika
- 6 cups boiling water
- 2 cups dry cornmeal
- 2 teaspoons salt

1. Use 1 tablespoon butter to lightly grease the inside of the crock pot. Sprinkle in paprika. Turn to high setting. 2. Add remaining ingredients to crock pot in the order listed, including 1 tablespoon butter. Stir well. 3. Cover and cook on high 2 to 3 hours, or on low 6 to 9 hours. Stir occasionally. 4. Pour hot cooked polenta into 2 lightly greased loaf pans. Chill 8 hours or overnight. 5. To serve, cut into ¼-inch-thick slices. Melt 2 tablespoons butter in large nonstick skillet, then lay in slices and cook until browned. Turn to brown other side. 6. For breakfast, serve with your choice of sweetener.

Cinnamon Buns

Prep time: 20 minutes | Cook time: 1½ hours | Serves 10 to 12

- Buns:
- 6 tablespoons unsalted butter, room temperature, plus more for brushing
- 1⅓ cups warm water (about 110°F / 43°C)
- 1 tablespoon active dry yeast
- 2 tablespoons honey
- 3½ cups all-purpose flour, plus more for work surface
- 2 teaspoon coarse salt
- ¾ cup granulated sugar
- ¼ cup plus 2 tablespoons packed brown sugar
- 1 tablespoon ground cinnamon
- Glaze:
- 3 cups confectioners' sugar
- Juice of ½ lemon
- 2 teaspoon vanilla extract
- ¼ cup plus 2 tablespoons milk

Make the Buns: 1. Brush the insert of a 5- to 6-quart crock pot with butter. Line bottom with parchment paper and brush paper with butter. 2. Combine the warm water, yeast, and honey in a bowl; let stand until foamy, about 5 minutes. Add flour and salt. With an electric mixer on low, mix until just combined. Increase speed to medium and mix for 5 minutes; let stand 10 minutes. Combine butter, both sugars, and cinnamon in a bowl; mix until smooth. 3. Preheat the crock pot. Turn dough out onto a lightly floured work surface and roll into a rectangle, about 9 by 15 inches. Sprinkle dough evenly with cinnamon-sugar mixture. Starting from one long side, roll into a log, pinching seams to seal in filling. Slice log into 10 to 12 rounds, each about 1½ inches thick. 4. Arrange rolls, cut side down, in the cooker. Wrap lid tightly with a clean kitchen towel, gathering ends at top (to absorb condensation). Cover and cook on high until cooked through, 1½ hours (we prefer to bake these on high). After 1 hour, rotate cooker insert to prevent scorching. Turn out onto a wire rack to cool before serving. Make the Glaze: 5. With an electric mixer, whisk confectioners' sugar, lemon juice, and vanilla until smooth. Slowly add ¼ cup milk and beat on medium. Add more milk, a drop at a time up to 2 tablespoons, to reach desired consistency. Drizzle rolls with glaze just before serving.

Peach French Toast Bake

Prep time: 15 minutes | Cook time: 6 hours | Serves 2

- Nonstick cooking spray
- ½ cup brown sugar
- 3 tablespoons butter
- 1 tablespoon water
- 1 teaspoon vanilla
- 8 slices French bread
- 1½ cups peeled sliced peaches
- 4 eggs
- 1 cup milk
- ¼ cup granulated sugar
- ½ teaspoon ground cinnamon
- ¼ teaspoon salt
- ⅔ cup chopped pecans

1. Line the crock pot with heavy-duty foil, and spray with the nonstick cooking spray. 2. In a small saucepan over low heat, bring the brown sugar, butter, and water to a simmer. Simmer about 5 minutes, stirring, until the mixture forms a syrup. Remove from the heat and stir in the vanilla. 3. In the crock pot, layer in the bread and the peaches, drizzling each layer with some of the brown sugar syrup. 4. In a medium bowl, beat the eggs, milk, granulated sugar, cinnamon, and salt. Pour the egg mixture into the crock pot and sprinkle with the pecans. 5. Cover and cook on low for 6 hours, or until the temperature registers 160°F (71°C) on a food thermometer and the mixture is set. 6. Remove from the crock pot, slice, and serve.

Basic Strata

Prep time: 10 minutes | Cook time: 4½ hours | Serves 8 to 10

- 8 cups torn or cubed (1-inch) stale bread, tough crusts removed
- 3½ to 4 cups shredded cheese
- 10 large eggs
- 3 cups milk
- 1½ teaspoons salt
- ½ teaspoon hot sauce

1. Coat the insert of a 5- to 7-quart crock pot with nonstick cooking spray or line it with a crock pot liner according to the manufacturer's directions. 2. Spread a layer of the bread into the crock pot and sprinkle with some of the cheese. Continue layering the bread and cheese until it has all been used, saving some cheese for the top. 3. Whisk together the eggs, milk, salt, and hot sauce in a large bowl. Pour the mixture over the cheese and bread and push it down to make sure the bread becomes saturated. Sprinkle the remaining cheese over the top. 4. Cover and cook on low for 4 hours, until the strata is cooked through (170°F / 77°C on an instant-read thermometer). Remove the lid and cook for an additional 30 minutes. 5. Serve the strata from the cooker set on warm.

Streusel Cake

Prep time: 10 minutes | Cook time: 3 to 4 hours | Serves 8 to 10

- 1 (16-ounce / 454-g) package pound cake mix, prepared according to package directions
- ¼ cup packed brown sugar
- 1 tablespoon flour
- ¼ cup chopped nuts
- 1 teaspoon cinnamon

1. Liberally grease and flour a 2-pound (907-g) coffee can, or crock pot baking insert, that fits into your crock pot. Pour prepared cake mix into coffee can or baking insert. 2. In a small bowl, mix brown sugar, flour, nuts, and cinnamon together. Sprinkle over top of cake mix. 3. Place coffee tin or baking insert in crock pot. Cover top of tin or insert with several layers of paper towels. 4. Cover cooker itself and cook on high 3 to 4 hours, or until toothpick inserted in center of cake comes out clean. 5. Remove baking tin from crock pot and allow to cool for 30 minutes before cutting into wedges to serve.

Sausage and Hash-Brown Casserole

Prep time: 25 minutes | Cook time: 2½ to 3 hours | Serves 8

- 1½ pounds (680 g) bulk pork sausage
- 2 medium onions, finely chopped
- 1 Anaheim chile, cored, seeded and finely chopped
- 1 medium red bell pepper, seeded and finely chopped
- 1 teaspoon ground cumin
- ½ teaspoon dried oregano
- 1 (16-ounce / 454-g) package frozen shredded hash brown potatoes,
- defrosted, or 2 cups fresh shredded hash browns
- 6 large eggs, beaten
- 1 cup milk
- 1 cup mayonnaise
- 1 cup prepared salsa (your choice of heat)
- 2 cups shredded mild Cheddar cheese, or 1 cup shredded mild Cheddar mixed with 1 cup shredded Pepper Jack cheese

1. Coat the insert of a 5- to 7-quart crock pot with nonstick cooking spray or line the insert with a crock pot liner according the manufacturer's directions. 2. Cook the sausage in a large skillet over high heat until it is no longer pink, breaking up any large pieces with the side of a spoon. 3. Remove all but 1 tablespoon of fat from the pan and heat over medium-high heat. Add the onions, chile, bell pepper, cumin, and oregano and sauté until the onions are softened and translucent, 5 to 6 minutes. Transfer the mixture to a bowl and allow to cool. 4. Add the potatoes to the bowl and stir to blend. In a smaller bowl, whisk together the eggs, milk, and mayonnaise. Pour over the sausage and potato mixture and stir to combine. 5. Transfer half the mixture to the crock pot insert, then cover with half the salsa and half the cheese. Repeat the layers with the remaining ingredients. Cover and cook on high for 2½ to 3

hours, until the casserole is puffed, and cooked through (170ºF / 77ºC on an instant-read thermometer). Remove the cover and allow the frittata to rest for 30 minutes. 6. Serve from the cooker set on warm.

Blueberry Fancy

Prep time: 15 minutes | Cook time: 3 to 4 hours | Serves 12

- 1 loaf Italian bread, cubed, divided
- 1 pint blueberries, divided
- 8 ounces (227 g) cream
- cheese, cubed, divided
- 6 eggs
- 1½ cups milk

1. Place half the bread cubes in the crock pot. 2. Drop half the blueberries over top the bread. 3. Sprinkle half the cream cheese cubes over the blueberries. 4. Repeat all 3 layers. 5. In a mixing bowl, whisk together eggs and milk. Pour over all ingredients. 6. Cover and cook on low until the dish is set. 7. Serve.

Easy Egg and Sausage Puff

Prep time: 15 minutes | Cook time: 2 to 2½ hours | Serves 6

- 1 pound (454 g) loose sausage
- 6 eggs
- 1 cup all-purpose baking mix
- 1 cup shredded Cheddar
- cheese
- 2 cups milk
- ¼ teaspoon dry mustard (optional)
- Nonstick cooking spray

1. Brown sausage in nonstick skillet. Break up chunks of meat as it cooks. Drain. 2. Meanwhile, spray interior of crock pot with nonstick cooking spray. 3. Mix all ingredients in crock pot. 4. Cover and cook on high 1 hour. Turn to low and cook 1 to 1½ hours, or until the dish is fully cooked in the center.

Bacon-and-Eggs Breakfast Casserole

Prep time: 15 minutes | Cook time: 5 to 6 hours | Serves 8

- 1 tablespoon bacon fat or extra-virgin olive oil
- 12 eggs
- 1 cup coconut milk
- 1 pound (454 g) bacon, chopped and cooked crisp
- ½ sweet onion, chopped
- 2 teaspoons minced garlic
- ¼ teaspoon freshly ground black pepper
- ⅛ teaspoon salt
- Pinch red pepper flakes

1. Lightly grease the insert of the crock pot with the bacon fat or olive oil. 2. In a medium bowl, whisk together the eggs, coconut milk, bacon, onion, garlic, pepper, salt, and red pepper flakes. Pour the mixture into the crock pot. 3. Cover and cook on low for 5 to 6 hours. 4. Serve warm.

Hot Wheat Berry Cereal

Prep time: 5 minutes | Cook time: 10 hours | Serves 4

- 1 cup wheat berries
- 5 cups water

1. Rinse and sort berries. Cover with water and soak all day (or 8 hours) in crock pot. 2. Cover. Cook on low overnight (or 10 hours). 3. Drain, if needed. Serve.

Hot Applesauce Breakfast

Prep time: 15 minutes | Cook time: 8 to 10 hours | Serves 8

- 10 apples, peeled and sliced
- ½ to 1 cup sugar
- 1 tablespoon ground
- cinnamon
- ¼ teaspoon ground nutmeg

1. Combine ingredients in crock pot. 2. Cover. Cook on low 8 to 10 hours.

Welsh Rarebit

Prep time: 10 minutes | Cook time: 1½ to 2½ hours | Serves 6 to 8

- 1 (12-ounce / 340-g) can beer
- 1 tablespoon dry mustard
- 1 teaspoon Worcestershire sauce
- ½ teaspoon salt
- ⅛ teaspoon black or white pepper
- 1 pound (454 g) American
- cheese, cubed
- 1 pound (454 g) sharp Cheddar cheese, cubed
- English muffins or toast
- Tomato slices
- Bacon, cooked until crisp
- Fresh steamed asparagus spears

1. In crock pot, combine beer, mustard, 2. Worcestershire sauce, salt, and pepper. Cover and cook on high 1 to 2 hours, until mixture boils. 3. Add cheese, a little at a time, stirring constantly until all the cheese melts. 4. Heat on high 20 to 30 minutes with cover off, stirring frequently. 5. Serve hot over toasted English muffins or over toasted bread cut into triangles. Garnish with tomato slices, strips of crisp bacon and steamed asparagus spears.

Dulce Leche

Prep time: 5 minutes | Cook time: 2 hours | Makes 2½ cups

- 2 (14-ounce / 397-g) cans sweetened condensed milk
- Cookies, for serving

1. Place unopened cans of milk in crock pot. Fill cooker with warm water so that it comes above the cans by 1½ to 2 inches. 2. Cover cooker. Cook on high 2 hours. 3. Cool unopened cans.

4. When opened, the contents should be thick and spreadable. Use as a filling between 2 cookies.

Slow-Cooked Blueberry French Toast

Prep time: 30 minutes | Cook time: 3 hours | Serves 12

- 8 eggs
- ½ cup plain yogurt
- ⅓ cup sour cream
- 1 teaspoon vanilla extract
- ½ teaspoon ground cinnamon
- 1 cup 2% milk
- ⅓ cup maple syrup
- 1 (1-pound / 454-g) loaf French bread, cubed
- 1½ cups fresh or frozen
- blueberries
- 12 ounces (340 g) cream cheese, cubed
- Blueberry Syrup:
- 1 cup sugar
- 2 tablespoons cornstarch
- 1 cup cold water
- ¾ cup fresh or frozen blueberries, divided
- 1 tablespoon butter
- 1 tablespoon lemon juice

1. In a large bowl, whisk eggs, yogurt, sour cream, vanilla and cinnamon. Gradually whisk in milk and maple syrup until blended. 2. Place half of the bread in a greased 5- or 6-quart crock pot; layer with half of the blueberries, cream cheese and egg mixture. Repeat layers. Refrigerate, covered, overnight. 3. Remove from refrigerator 30 minutes before cooking. Cook, covered, on low 3 to 4 hours or until a knife inserted near the center comes out clean. 4. For syrup, in a small saucepan, mix sugar and cornstarch; stir in water until smooth. Stir in ¼ cup blueberries. Bring to a boil; cook and stir until berries pop, about 3 minutes. Remove from heat; stir in butter, lemon juice and remaining berries. Serve warm with French toast.

Slow-Cooked Fruited Oatmeal with Nuts

Prep time: 15 minutes | Cook time: 6 hours | Serves 6

- 3 cups water
- 2 cups old-fashioned oats
- 2 cups chopped apples
- 1 cup dried cranberries
- 1 cup fat-free milk
- 2 teaspoons butter, melted
- 1 teaspoon pumpkin pie spice
- 1 teaspoon ground cinnamon
- 6 tablespoons chopped almonds, toasted
- 6 tablespoons chopped pecans, toasted
- Additional fat-free milk

1. In a 3-quart crock pot coated with cooking spray, combine the first eight ingredients. Cover and cook on low for 6 to 8 hours or until liquid is absorbed. 2. Spoon oatmeal into bowls. Sprinkle with almonds and pecans; drizzle with additional milk if desired.

Summer Squash and Mushroom Strata

Prep time: 20 minutes | Cook time: 6 hours | Serves 2

- 1 onion, chopped
- 2 garlic cloves, minced
- 1½ cups sliced cremini mushrooms
- 1 red bell pepper, chopped
- 1 yellow summer squash, chopped
- Nonstick cooking spray
- 6 slices French bread, cubed
- 1 cup shredded Cheddar cheese
- 1 cup shredded Swiss cheese
- 5 eggs, beaten
- 1 cup milk
- 1 tablespoon Dijon mustard
- ½ teaspoon salt
- ½ teaspoon dried basil leaves
- ⅛ teaspoon freshly ground black pepper

1. In a medium bowl, mix the onion, garlic, mushrooms, bell pepper, and squash. 2. Spray the crock pot with the nonstick cooking spray. 3. In the crock pot, layer the bread, vegetable mixture, and Cheddar and Swiss cheeses. 4. In a medium bowl, beat the eggs, milk, mustard, salt, basil, and pepper until combined. 5. Pour the egg mixture into the crock pot. 6. Cover and cook on low for 6 hours, or until the temperature registers 160°F (71°C) on a food thermometer. 7. Cut into squares and serve.

Zucchini-Carrot Bread

Prep time: 15 minutes | Cook time: 3 to 5 hours | Makes 8 slices

- 2 teaspoons butter, for greasing pan
- 1 cup almond flour
- 1 cup granulated erythritol
- ½ cup coconut flour
- 1½ teaspoons baking powder
- 1 teaspoon ground cinnamon
- ½ teaspoon ground nutmeg
- ½ teaspoon baking soda
- ¼ teaspoon salt
- 4 eggs
- ½ cup butter, melted
- 1 tablespoon pure vanilla extract
- 1½ cups finely grated zucchini
- ½ cup finely grated carrot

1. Lightly grease a 9-by-5-inch loaf pan with the butter and set aside. 2. Place a small rack in the bottom of your crock pot. 3. In a large bowl, stir together the almond flour, erythritol, coconut flour, baking powder, cinnamon, nutmeg, baking soda, and salt until well mixed. 4. In a separate medium bowl, whisk together the eggs, melted butter, and vanilla until well blended. 5. Add the wet ingredients to dry ingredients and stir to combine. 6. Stir in the zucchini and carrot. 7. Spoon the batter into the prepared loaf pan. 8. Place the loaf pan on the rack in the bottom of the crock pot, cover, and cook on high for 3 hours. 9. Remove the loaf pan, let the bread cool completely, and serve.

Sausage Quiche

Prep time: 20 minutes | Cook time: 6 hours | Serves 2

- 8 ounces (227 g) pork sausage
- 1 onion, chopped
- 1 cup sliced mushrooms
- Nonstick baking spray containing flour
- 2 garlic cloves, minced
- 1 red bell pepper, chopped
- 1 cup shredded Cheddar cheese, divided
- 4 eggs, beaten
- 1 cup whole milk
- ½ cup all-purpose flour
- ½ teaspoon baking powder
- ½ teaspoon salt
- ½ teaspoon dried basil leaves
- ⅛ teaspoon freshly ground black pepper
- ⅓ cup grated Parmesan cheese

1. In a medium saucepan over medium heat, cook the sausage with the onions, stirring to break up the meat, until the sausage is browned, about 10 minutes. Drain well and add the mushrooms; cook, stirring, until the mushrooms give up their liquid and the liquid evaporates, about 5 minutes. 2. Line the crock pot with heavy-duty foil. Spray the foil with the nonstick baking spray containing flour. 3. In the crock pot, layer the sausage mixture, garlic, and bell pepper. Top with ½ cup of Cheddar cheese. 4. In a medium bowl, beat the eggs, milk, flour, baking powder, salt, basil, and pepper. Pour the egg mixture into the crock pot and top with the remaining ½ cup of Cheddar cheese. Sprinkle with the Parmesan cheese. 5. Cover and cook on low for 6 hours, or until the quiche registers 160°F (71°C) on a food thermometer, the edges are browned, and the center is set. 6. Remove from the crock pot and let stand for 5 minutes; cut into wedges and serve.

Egg and Broccoli Casserole

Prep time: 15 minutes | Cook time: 2½ to 3 hours | Serves 6

- 1 (24-ounce / 680-g) carton small-curd cottage cheese
- 1 (10-ounce / 283-g) package frozen chopped broccoli, thawed and drained
- 2 cups shredded Cheddar cheese
- 6 eggs, beaten
- ⅓ cup flour
- ¼ cup butter, melted
- 3 tablespoons finely chopped onion
- ½ teaspoon salt
- Shredded cheese (optional)

1. Combine first 8 ingredients. Pour into greased crock pot. 2. Cover and cook on high 1 hour. Stir. Reduce heat to low. Cover and cook 2½ to 3 hours, or until temperature reaches 160°F (71°C) and eggs are set. 3. Sprinkle with cheese and serve.

Breakfast Fruit Compote

Prep time: 5 minutes | Cook time: 2 to 7 hours | Serves 8 to 9

- 1 (12-ounce / 340-g) package dried apricots
- 1 (12-ounce / 340-g) package pitted dried plums
- 1 (11-ounce / 312-g) can mandarin oranges in light syrup, undrained
- 1 (29-ounce / 822-g) can sliced peaches in light syrup, undrained
- ¼ cup white raisins
- 10 maraschino cherries

1. Combine all ingredients in crock pot. Mix well. 2. Cover. Cook on low 6 to 7 hours, or on high 2 to 3 hours.

Chapter 2
Beans and Grains

Garbanzos Tuscan-Style

Prep time: 15 minutes | Cook time: 6 to 7 hours | Serves 6 to 8

- 2 tablespoons extra-virgin olive oil
- 3 cloves garlic, minced
- 1 medium onion, finely chopped
- 2 teaspoons fresh rosemary leaves, finely chopped
- 2 (14- to 15-ounce / 397- to 425-g) cans crushed tomatoes
- 2 tablespoons dry red wine
- 4 (14- to 15-ounce / 397- to 425-g) cans garbanzo beans, rinsed and drained
- 1½ teaspoons salt
- ½ teaspoon freshly ground black pepper
- ½ cup finely chopped fresh Italian parsley

1. Heat the oil in a medium skillet over medium-high heat. Add the garlic, onion, and rosemary and sauté until the onion is softened, about 3 minutes. Add the tomatoes and wine and swirl in the pan to combine. 2. Transfer the contents of the skillet to the insert of a 5- to 7-quart crock pot and stir in the beans along with the salt and pepper. Cover and cook on low for 6 to 7 hours, until the beans are soft and creamy. 3. Stir in the parsley and serve.

"Lean" Cowboy Beans

Prep time: 15 minutes | Cook time: 1 to 2 hours | Serves 8

- 1 pound (454 g) ground turkey
- 1 (16-ounce / 454-g) can baked beans, undrained
- 1 (16-ounce / 454-g) can kidney beans, drained
- 2 cups onions, chopped
- ¾ cup brown sugar
- 1 cup ketchup
- 2 tablespoons dry mustard
- ¼ teaspoon salt
- 2 teaspoons cider vinegar

1. Brown turkey in nonstick skillet over medium heat. 2. Combine all ingredients in crock pot sprayed with nonfat cooking spray. 3. Cover. Cook on high 1 to 2 hours.

Scandinavian Beans

Prep time: 50 minutes | Cook time: 8 hours | Serves 8

- 1 pound (454 g) dried pinto beans
- 6 cups water
- 12 ounces (340 g) bacon, or 1 ham hock
- 1 onion, chopped
- 2 to 3 garlic cloves, minced
- ¼ teaspoon pepper
- 1 teaspoon salt
- ¼ cup molasses
- 1 cup ketchup
- Tabasco to taste
- 1 teaspoon Worcestershire sauce
- ¾ cup brown sugar
- ½ cup cider vinegar
- ¼ teaspoon dry mustard

1. Soak beans in water in soup pot for 8 hours. Bring beans to boil and cook 1½ to 2 hours, or until soft. Drain, reserving liquid. 2. Combine all ingredients in crock pot, using just enough bean liquid to cover everything. Cook on low 5 to 6 hours. If using ham hock, debone, cut ham into bite-sized pieces, and mix into beans.

Rice and Turkey crock pot Bake

Prep time: 15 minutes | Cook time: 3 to 8 hours | Serves 6

- 1½ pounds (680 g) ground turkey
- 1 teaspoon sea salt
- ½ teaspoon black pepper
- 2 tablespoons chopped fresh thyme
- 2 tablespoons chopped fresh sage
- 2 cups converted brown rice
- 2 cups chicken stock (or turkey stock if you have it)
- 1 tablespoon plus 1 teaspoon balsamic vinegar
- 1 medium yellow onion, chopped
- 2 garlic cloves, minced
- 1 (14-ounce / 397-g) can stewed tomatoes, with the juice
- 3 medium-size zucchini, sliced thinly
- ¼ cup pitted and sliced Kalamata olives
- ¼ cup chopped fresh flat-leaf parsley
- ½ cup grated Parmigiano-Reggiano cheese, for serving (optional)

1. Spray a large skillet with cooking oil spray. Place over medium-high heat. Add the ground turkey, 1 teaspoon salt, ½ teaspoon pepper, 1 tablespoon of the thyme, and 1 tablespoon of the sage. Sauté until turkey is no longer pink. Drain off the fat, and place the turkey mixture into the crock pot. 2. Add the rice, chicken stock, and vinegar and stir to combine. Add the onion, garlic, tomatoes, zucchini, and olives and stir. Add the remaining 1 tablespoon thyme, remaining 1 tablespoon sage, and parsley. Mix well. 3. Cover and cook on low for 6 to 8 hours, or on high for 3 to 4 hours. 4. Season with additional salt and pepper if needed. Serve hot with Parmigiano-Reggiano cheese sprinkled on top, if desired.

From-Scratch Baked Beans

Prep time: 10 minutes | Cook time: 14 hours | Serves 6

- 2½ cups Great Northern dried beans
- 4 cups water
- 1½ cups tomato sauce
- ½ cup brown sugar
- 2 teaspoons salt
- 1 small onion, chopped
- ½ teaspoon chili powder

1. Wash and drain dry beans. Combine beans and water in crock pot. Cook on low 8 hours, or overnight. 2. Stir in remaining ingredients. Cook on low 6 hours. If the beans look too watery as they near the end of their cooking time, you can remove the lid during the last 30 to 60 minutes.

Risi Bisi (Peas and Rice)

Prep time: 15 minutes | Cook time: 2½ to 3½ hours | Serves 6

- 1½ cups converted long-grain white rice, uncooked
- ¾ cup chopped onions
- 2 garlic cloves, minced
- 2 (14½-ounce / 411-g) cans reduced-sodium chicken broth
- ⅓ cup water
- ¾ teaspoon Italian seasoning
- ½ teaspoon dried basil leaves
- ½ cup frozen baby peas, thawed
- ¼ cup grated Parmesan cheese

1. Combine rice, onions, and garlic in crock pot. 2. In saucepan, mix together chicken broth and water. Bring to boil. Add Italian seasoning and basil leaves. Stir into rice mixture. 3. Cover. Cook on low 2 to 3 hours, or until liquid is absorbed. 4. Stir in peas. Cover. Cook 30 minutes. Stir in cheese.

Asparagus Risotto

Prep time: 15 minutes | Cook time: 5½ hours | Serves 2

- Nonstick cooking spray
- 1½ cups Arborio rice
- 1 leek, white and light green parts only, sliced
- 2 garlic cloves, minced
- ¼ cup dry white wine
- 4 cups vegetable broth
- ½ teaspoon salt
- ⅛ teaspoon freshly ground black pepper
- ½ pound (227 g) asparagus
- ½ cup grated Parmesan cheese
- 1 tablespoon butter

1. Spray the crock pot with the nonstick cooking spray. 2. In the crock pot, combine the rice, leek, garlic, wine, broth, salt, and pepper, and stir. 3. Cover and cook on low for 5 hours, or until the rice is tender. Stir well. 4. Wash and trim the asparagus, and cut it into 1-inch lengths. 5. Add the asparagus to the crock pot; cover and cook on high for 30 minutes, or until the asparagus is crisp-tender. 6. Stir in the cheese and butter. Cover and let stand for 5 minutes, then serve.

Risotto alla Milanese

Prep time: 10 minutes | Cook time: 2½ hours | Serves 4 to 6

- ½ cup (1 stick) unsalted butter
- 2 tablespoons olive oil
- 1 teaspoon saffron threads
- ½ cup finely chopped shallots (about 4 medium)
- 1½ cups Arborio or
- Carnaroli rice
- ¼ cup dry white wine or vermouth
- 4 cups chicken broth
- ½ cup freshly grated Parmigiano-Reggiano cheese

1. Coat the insert of a 5- to 7-quart crock pot with nonstick cooking spray or line it with a crock pot liner according to the manufacturer's directions. 2. Melt ¼ cup of the butter with the oil in a large saucepan over medium-high heat. Add the saffron and shallots and cook, stirring, until the shallots are softened. Add the rice and cook, coating the rice with the butter, until the rice begins to look opaque. Add the wine and allow it to evaporate. 3. Transfer the contents of the saucepan to the crock pot insert. Add the broth and stir to incorporate it. Cover and cook on high for 2½ hours; check the risotto at 2 hours to make sure that the broth hasn't evaporated. At the end of the cooking time, the risotto should be tender and creamy. Stir in the remaining ¼ cup butter and ¼ cup of the cheese. 4. Serve the risotto with the remaining cheese on the side.

Bulgur with Basil, Mint, and Tomato

Prep time: 15 minutes | Cook time: 5 to 6 hours | Serves 8

- 2 cups medium bulgur
- 2 tablespoons extra-virgin olive oil
- 1 medium onion, finely chopped
- 3 cloves garlic, minced
- Pinch of red pepper flakes
- 1 (14- to 15-ounce / 397- to 425-g) can chopped
- tomatoes, drained but juice reserved
- 3½ cups chicken or vegetable broth
- 1 teaspoon salt
- ¼ cup finely chopped fresh basil
- ¼ cup finely chopped fresh mint

1. Coat the insert of a 5- to 7-quart crock pot with nonstick cooking spray and add the bulgur. Heat the oil in a large skillet over medium-high heat. Add the onion, garlic, and red pepper flakes and sauté until the onion is softened, about 3 minutes. Add the drained tomatoes and cook until there is no liquid left in the pan. 2. Pour the broth in the skillet and scrape up any browned bits on the bottom of the pan. Transfer the contents of the skillet to the crock pot insert and stir in the reserved tomato juice and the salt. Cover and cook on low for 5 to 6 hours, until the bulgur is tender and the liquid is absorbed. 3. Stir in the basil and mint and serve from the cooker set on warm.

Moroccan Oatmeal

Prep time: 5 minutes | Cook time: 3 hours | Serves 4

- 3 cups water or milk, any kind you prefer
- 1 cup steel-cut oats
- ½ teaspoon sea salt
- 1 teaspoon ground
- cinnamon
- ½ cup any combination of diced dried apricots, dates, figs, and raisins (raisins can be whole)

1. Combine the water or milk and the oats in the crock pot. Sprinkle in the salt and cinnamon. 2. Add the dried fruit to the mixture. Cover and cook on low heat for 3 hours. Do not open and/or stir until the cooking time has elapsed and the oats are cooked. 3. Serve hot.

Lotsa-Beans Pot

Prep time: 30 minutes | Cook time: 3 to 4 hours | Serves 15 to 20

- 8 bacon strips, diced
- 2 onions, thinly sliced
- 1 cup packed brown sugar
- ½ cup cider vinegar
- 1 teaspoon salt
- 1 teaspoon ground mustard
- ½ teaspoon garlic powder
- 1 (28-ounce / 794-g) can baked beans
- 1 (16-ounce / 454-g) can kidney beans, rinsed and drained
- 1 (15½-ounce / 439-g) can pinto beans, rinsed and drained
- 1 (15-ounce / 425-g) can lima beans, rinsed and drained
- 1 (15½-ounce / 439-g) can black-eyed peas, rinsed and drained

1. Cook bacon in skillet until crisp. Remove to paper towels. 2. Drain, reserving 2 tablespoons drippings. 3. Sauté onions in drippings until tender. 4. Add brown sugar, vinegar, salt, mustard, and garlic powder to skillet. Bring to boil. 5. Combine beans and peas in crock pot. Add onion mixture and bacon. Mix well. 6. Cover. Cook on high 3 to 4 hours.

Arroz con Queso

Prep time: 15 minutes | Cook time: 6 to 9 hours | Serves 6 to 8

- 1 (14½-ounce / 411-g) can whole tomatoes, mashed
- 1 (15-ounce / 425-g) can Mexican style beans, undrained
- 1½ cups long-grain rice, uncooked
- 1 cup shredded Monterey Jack cheese
- 1 large onion, finely chopped
- 1 cup cottage cheese
- 1 (4¼-ounce / 120-g) can chopped green chili peppers, drained
- 1 tablespoon oil
- 3 garlic cloves, minced
- 1 teaspoon salt
- 1 cup shredded Monterey Jack cheese

1. Combine all ingredients except final cup of cheese. Pour into well greased crock pot. 2. Cover. Cook on low 6 to 9 hours. 3. Sprinkle with remaining cheese before serving.

White Beans with Kale

Prep time: 15 minutes | Cook time: 7½ hours | Serves 2

- 1 onion, chopped
- 1 leek, white part only, sliced
- 2 celery stalks, sliced
- 2 garlic cloves, minced
- 1 cup dried white lima beans or cannellini beans, sorted and rinsed
- 2 cups vegetable broth
- ½ teaspoon salt
- ½ teaspoon dried thyme leaves
- ⅛ teaspoon freshly ground black pepper
- 3 cups torn kale

1. In the crock pot, combine all the ingredients except the kale.

2. Cover and cook on low for 7 hours, or until the beans are tender. 3. Add the kale and stir. 4. Cover and cook on high for 30 minutes, or until the kale is tender but still firm, and serve.

Hometown Spanish Rice

Prep time: 20 minutes | Cook time: 2 to 4 hours | Serves 6 to 8

- 1 large onion, chopped
- 1 bell pepper, chopped
- 1 pound (454 g) bacon, cooked, and broken into bite-size pieces
- 2 cups long-grain rice, cooked
- 1 (28-ounce / 794-g) can stewed tomatoes with juice
- Grated Parmesan cheese (optional)
- Nonstick cooking spray

1. Sauté onion and pepper in a small nonstick frying pan until tender. 2. Spray interior of crock pot with nonstick cooking spray. 3. Combine all ingredients in the crock pot. 4. Cover and cook on low 4 hours, or on high 2 hours, or until heated through. 5. Sprinkle with Parmesan cheese just before serving, if you wish.

Mediterranean Rice and Sausage

Prep time: 10 minutes | Cook time: 2 to 5 hours | Serves 4

- ¼ cup olive oil, plus 1 tablespoon
- 1½ cups uncooked brown rice
- 1 large yellow onion, chopped
- 2 cloves garlic, minced
- ½ green bell pepper, chopped
- ¾ pound (340 g) bulk
- ground Italian sausage
- 4 cups tomato juice
- 1 teaspoon Worcestershire sauce
- ½ cup red wine of your choice
- ½ teaspoon cayenne pepper
- 1 teaspoon sea salt
- ¼ teaspoon black pepper

1. Heat ¼ cup of the olive oil over medium-high heat in a medium skillet. Add the brown rice and brown, tossing frequently, for 2 to 3 minutes. Remove the rice to a small bowl and set aside. 2. In same skillet, heat the remaining 1 tablespoon olive oil over medium-high heat. Add the onion and garlic and sauté for 1 or 2 minutes until fragrant. 3. Add the bell pepper. Cook for 2 or 3 minutes until the bell pepper has softened. Remove the vegetables to a small bowl and set aside. 4. Add the Italian sausage to the skillet. Cook over medium-high heat until just browned, about 4 minutes. Remove from the heat. 5. In a blender or food processor, purée one-half of the vegetable mix, which should now be just cool enough to handle, until just smooth. 6. To the crock pot, add the tomato juice, Worcestershire sauce, red wine, puréed vegetables, and cooked vegetables. Add browned rice. Add the browned Italian sausage. Sprinkle in the cayenne pepper, 1 teaspoon salt, and ¼ teaspoon pepper. 7. Cover and cook on high for 2 hours. Switch to low heat and continue cooking for 5 hours. 8. Season with additional salt and pepper, as needed. Serve hot.

Cheddar Rice

Prep time: 15 minutes | Cook time: 2 to 3 hours | Serves 8 to 10

- 2 cups brown rice, uncooked
- 3 tablespoons butter
- ½ cup thinly sliced green onions or shallots
- 1 teaspoon salt
- 5 cups water
- ½ teaspoon pepper
- 2 cups shredded Cheddar cheese
- 1 cup slivered almonds (optional)

1. Combine rice, butter, green onion, and salt in crock pot. 2. Bring water to boil and pour over rice mixture. 3. Cover and cook on high 2 to 3 hours, or until rice is tender and liquid is absorbed. 4. Five minutes before serving stir in pepper and cheese. 5. Garnish with slivered almonds, if you wish.

Cowboy Beans

Prep time: 20 minutes | Cook time: 3 to 7 hours | Serves 10 to 12

- 6 slices bacon, cut in pieces
- ½ cup onions, chopped
- 1 garlic clove, minced
- 1 (16-ounce / 454-g) can baked beans
- 1 (16-ounce / 454-g) can kidney beans, drained
- 1 (15-ounce / 425-g) can butter beans or pinto beans, drained
- 2 tablespoons dill pickle relish or chopped dill pickles
- ⅓ cup chili sauce or ketchup
- 2 teaspoons Worcestershire sauce
- ½ cup brown sugar
- ⅛ teaspoon hot pepper sauce (optional)

1. Lightly brown bacon, onions, and garlic in skillet. Drain. 2. Combine all ingredients in crock pot. Mix well. 3. Cover. Cook on low 5 to 7 hours, or on high 3 to 4 hours.

Chicken Sausage Cassoulet

Prep time: 10 minutes | Cook time: 3 to 8 hours | Serves 6

- Nonstick cooking oil spray
- 1 large yellow onion, chopped
- ¾ cup baby carrots, halved lengthwise
- 2 tablespoons garlic, minced
- 1¼ pounds (567 g) chicken or turkey sausage, cut into 2-inch sections
- 2 (8-ounce / 227-g) cans tomato sauce
- 1 tablespoon dried herbs de Provence
- 1 teaspoon black pepper
- 2 (15-ounce / 425-g) cans great northern beans, drained and rinsed
- 4 slices bacon, cooked and crumbled

1. Coat the inside of the crock pot crock with cooking oil spray. Add the onion, carrots, garlic, sausage, and tomato sauce. Sprinkle with the herbes de Provence and pepper. Stir to combine. 2. Cover and cook on low for 7 to 8 hours or high for 3½ to 4 hours. Add the beans to the pot in the last hour of

cooking. 3. Serve hot, with bacon sprinkled on each serving.

Kale with Chickpeas

Prep time: 10 minutes | Cook time: 4 to 6 hours | Serves 6

- 1 to 2 tablespoons rapeseed oil
- ½ teaspoon mustard seeds
- 1 teaspoon cumin seeds
- 1 large onion, diced
- 4 garlic cloves, crushed
- 4 plum tomatoes, finely chopped
- 1 heaped teaspoon coriander seeds, ground
- 1 fresh green chile, chopped
- 1 teaspoon chili powder
- 1 teaspoon turmeric
- 1 teaspoon salt
- 2 (16-ounce / 454-g) cans cooked chickpeas, drained and rinsed
- ¾ cup water
- 7 to 8 ounces (198 to 227 g) kale, chopped
- 1 fresh green chile, sliced, for garnish

1. Heat the oil in a frying pan (or in the crock pot if you have a sear setting). When it's hot add the mustard seeds and then the cumin seeds until they pop and become fragrant. 2. Add the diced onion and cook, stirring, for 10 minutes. Add the garlic and cook for a few minutes. Then add the tomatoes. Add the ground coriander seeds, green chile, chili powder, turmeric, and salt. 3. Add the chickpeas and water. Cover and cook on low for 6 hours, or on high for 4 hours. 4. Add the chopped kale, a handful at a time, stirring between. Leave this to cook for another 10 to 15 minutes, until the kale is soft and tender. 5. Top with the sliced chile.

Risotto with Gorgonzola

Prep time: 10 minutes | Cook time: 2½ hours | Serves 4 to 6

- ½ cup (1 stick) unsalted butter
- 2 tablespoons olive oil
- ½ cup finely chopped shallots (about 4 medium)
- 1½ cups Arborio or
- Carnaroli rice
- ¼ cup dry white wine or vermouth
- 4 cups chicken broth
- 1 cup crumbled Gorgonzola cheese

1. Coat the insert of a 5- to 7-quart crock pot with nonstick cooking spray or line it with a crock pot liner according to the manufacturer's directions. 2. Heat ¼ cup of the butter with the oil in a large saucepan over medium-high heat. Add the shallots and sauté until softened, about 4 minutes. Add the rice and cook, stirring to coat with the butter, until the rice begins to look opaque. Add the wine and cook until the wine evaporates. 3. Transfer the mixture to the crock pot insert and stir in the broth. Cover and cook on high for 2½ hours; check the risotto at 2 hours to make sure that the broth hasn't evaporated. 4. Stir in the remaining butter and Gorgonzola before serving immediately.

Chapter 3

Beef, Pork, and Lamb

Pork Shoulder Shanghai-Style

Prep time: 20 minutes | Cook time: 6 hours | Serves 6 to 8

- 1 cup soy sauce
- 1 cup rice wine (mirin) or dry sherry
- ½ cup firmly packed light brown sugar
- ½ cup ketchup
- ½ teaspoon five-spice powder
- 2 cloves garlic, minced
- 1 teaspoon freshly grated ginger
- 1 (3- to 4-pound / 1.4- to 1.8-kg) boneless pork shoulder, tied with kitchen string
- 2 tablespoons cornstarch mixed with ¼ cup water

1. Combine the soy sauce, rice wine, sugar, ketchup, five-spice powder, garlic, and ginger in a large zipper-top plastic bag. Add the pork to the bag, seal, and turn to coat the meat with the marinade. Refrigerate for at least 8 hours or up to 24 hours. 2. Pour the meat and marinade into the insert of a 5- to 7-quart crock pot. Cover and cook on high for 5 to 6 hours, until the meat is tender. Remove the meat from the crock pot and allow to rest for 15 minutes. 3. Shred the meat using two forks. Skim off the fat from the sauce and stir in the cornstarch mixture. Return the meat to the sauce, cover, and cook for an additional 30 minutes, until the sauce is thickened. 4. Serve the pork from the crock pot set on warm.

Conga Lime Pork

Prep time: 20 minutes | Cook time: 4 hours | Serves 6

- 1 teaspoon salt, divided
- ½ teaspoon pepper, divided
- 1 (2- to 3-pound / 907-g to 1.4-kg) boneless pork shoulder butt roast
- 1 tablespoon canola oil
- 1 large onion, chopped
- 3 garlic cloves, peeled and thinly sliced
- ½ cup water
- 2 chipotle peppers in adobo
- sauce, seeded and chopped
- 2 tablespoons molasses
- 2 cups broccoli coleslaw mix
- 1 medium mango, peeled and chopped
- 2 tablespoons lime juice
- 1½ teaspoons grated lime peel
- 6 prepared corn muffins, halved

1. Sprinkle ¾ teaspoon salt and ¼ teaspoon pepper over roast. In a large skillet, brown pork in oil on all sides. Transfer meat to a 3- or 4-quart crock pot. 2. In the same skillet, saute onion until tender. Add garlic; cook 1 minute longer. Add water, chipotle peppers and molasses, stirring to loosen browned bits from pan. Pour over pork. Cover and cook on high for 4 to 5 hours or until meat is tender. 3. Remove roast; cool slightly. Skim fat from cooking juices. Shred pork with two forks and return to crock pot; heat through. In a large bowl, combine the coleslaw mix, mango, lime juice, lime peel and remaining salt and pepper. 4. Place muffin halves cut side down on an ungreased baking sheet. Broil 4 inch from the heat for 2 to 3 minutes or until lightly toasted. Serve pork with muffins; top with slaw.

Tortilla Casserole

Prep time: 20 minutes | Cook time: 3¼ to 4¼ hours | Serves 4

- 4 to 6 white or whole wheat tortillas, divided
- 1 pound (454 g) ground beef
- 1 envelope dry taco seasoning
- 1 (16-ounce / 454-g) can
- fat-free refried beans
- 1½ cups shredded low-fat cheese of your choice, divided
- 3 to 4 tablespoons sour cream (optional)
- Nonstick cooking spray

1. Spray the inside of the cooker with nonstick cooking spray. Tear about ¾ of the tortillas into pieces and line the sides and bottom of the crock pot. 2. Brown the ground beef in a nonstick skillet. Drain. Return to skillet and mix in taco seasoning. 3. Layer refried beans, browned and seasoned meat, 1 cup cheese, and sour cream if you wish, over tortilla pieces. 4. Place remaining tortilla pieces on top. 5. Sprinkle with remaining cheese. Cover and cook on low 3 to 4 hours.

Creamy Hamburger Topping

Prep time: 15 minutes | Cook time: 3 to 5 hours | Serves 8

- 1 pound (454 g) ground beef
- 8 ounces (227 g) shredded cheese, your choice of flavors
- 1 onion, diced
- 1 (10¾-ounce / 305-g) can cream of mushroom soup
- 1 (12-ounce / 340-g) can diced tomatoes, undrained

1. Brown ground beef in a nonstick skillet. Drain. 2. Combine all ingredients in your crock pot. 3. Cook on low 3 to 5 hours, or until heated through. 4. Serve.

Slow-Cooked Pork Chops with Green Beans

Prep time: 10 minutes | Cook time: 4 to 8 hours | Serves 3 to 4

- 3 to 4 boneless pork chops
- Salt and pepper to taste
- 2 cups green beans, frozen or fresh
- 2 slices bacon, cut up
- ½ cup water
- 1 tablespoon lemon juice

1. Place pork chops in bottom of crock pot. Sprinkle with salt and pepper to taste. 2. Top with remaining ingredients in the order listed. 3. Cover and cook on low 4 to 8 hours, or until meat and green beans are tender but not dry or overcooked.

Just-Peachy Pork Chops

Prep time: 20 minutes | Cook time: 3 to 6 hours | Serves 6

- ¼ cup all-purpose flour
- Salt and freshly ground black pepper
- 4 tablespoons (½ stick) unsalted butter
- 6 center-cut, bone-in, 1-inch-thick pork chops
- 2 cups cipollini or small pearl onions, peeled and left whole
- 2 teaspoons dried sage
- leaves, crumbled in the palm of your hand
- 2 tablespoons light brown sugar
- 1 cup peach preserves
- ¼ cup balsamic vinegar
- ¼ cup beef broth, plus ¼ cup (optional)
- 2 tablespoons cornstarch (optional)

1. Combine the flour, 2 teaspoons salt, and 1 teaspoon pepper in a shallow dish. Dip each chop in the flour, coating both sides lightly and shaking off any excess flour. Melt 2 tablespoons of the butter in a large skillet over medium heat. Add half the chops and brown on both sides. Repeat with the remaining chops. 2. Transfer the chops to the insert of a 5- to 7-quart crock pot. Melt the remaining 2 tablespoons butter in the same skillet. Add the onions, sage, and sugar and sauté until the onions begin to turn golden, about 10 minutes. Add the preserves, vinegar, and ¼ cup broth and stir to blend. 3. Cover the chops with the onion mixture. Cover the crock pot and cook on high for 3 hours or on low for 6 hours. Remove the cover from the crock pot. Season with salt and pepper. (If you would like to thicken the sauce, mix 2 tablespoons cornstarch with ¼ cup beef broth. Thirty minutes before the chops are done, remove the cover and stir in the cornstarch mixture. Cover the cooker and cook on high for an additional 30 minutes, until the sauce is thickened.) 4. Serve the chops napped with some of the sauce and onions.

Sesame Pork Ribs

Prep time: 20 minutes | Cook time: 5 to 6 hours | Serves 6

- 1 medium onion, sliced
- ¾ cup packed brown sugar
- ¼ cup soy sauce
- ½ cup ketchup
- ¼ cup honey
- 2 tablespoons cider or white vinegar
- 3 garlic cloves, minced
- 1 teaspoon ground ginger
- ¼ to ½ teaspoon crushed red pepper flakes
- 5 pounds (2.3 kg) country-style pork ribs
- 2 tablespoons sesame seeds, toasted
- 2 tablespoons chopped green onions

1. Place onions in bottom of crock pot. 2. Combine brown sugar, soy sauce, ketchup, honey, vinegar, garlic, ginger, and red pepper flakes in large bowl. Add ribs and turn to coat. Place on top of onions in crock pot. Pour sauce over meat. 3. Cover.

Cook on low 5 to 6 hours. 4. Place ribs on serving platter. Sprinkle with sesame seeds and green onions. Serve sauce on the side.

Chuck Wagon Beef

Prep time: 20 minutes | Cook time: 8¼ to 10¼ hours | Serves 8

- 1 (4-pound / 1.8-kg) boneless chuck roast
- 1 teaspoon garlic salt
- ¼ teaspoon black pepper
- 2 tablespoons oil
- 6 to 8 garlic cloves, minced
- 1 large onion, sliced
- 1 cup water
- 1 bouillon cube
- 2 to 3 teaspoons instant coffee
- 1 bay leaf, or 1 tablespoon mixed Italian herbs
- 3 tablespoons cold water
- 2 tablespoons cornstarch

1. Sprinkle roast with garlic salt and pepper. Brown on all sides in oil in saucepan. Place in crock pot. 2. Sauté garlic and onion in meat drippings in saucepan. Add water, bouillon cube, and coffee. Cook over low heat for several minutes, stirring until drippings loosen. Pour over meat in cooker. 3. Add bay leaf or herbs. 4. Cover. Cook on low 8 to 10 hours, or until very tender. Remove bay leaf and discard. Remove meat to serving platter and keep warm. 5. Mix water and cornstarch together until paste forms. Stir into hot liquid and onions in cooker. Cover. Cook 10 minutes on high, or until thickened. 6. Slice meat before serving.

Lamb Marsala

Prep time: 15 minutes | Cook time: 9 hours | Serves 2

- 2 tablespoons extra-virgin olive oil
- 2 lamb shanks, trimmed and cracked
- ½ teaspoon salt
- ⅛ teaspoon freshly ground black pepper
- ½ cup chicken stock
- 1 leek, white part only,
- chopped
- 2 carrots, sliced
- 2 garlic cloves, minced
- 1 (14 ounces / 397 g) can diced tomatoes, undrained
- 1 cup Marsala wine
- 2 teaspoons minced fresh rosemary leaves

1. In a large saucepan over medium heat, heat the oil. 2. Sprinkle the lamb with the salt and pepper, add it to the pan, and brown it on all sides, turning several times, about 5 minutes. 3. Remove the lamb from the saucepan to a platter, and add the stock to the pan. Bring the stock to a simmer, scraping up the pan drippings. Remove from the heat. 4. In the crock pot, combine the leek, carrots, garlic, and tomatoes. Top with the lamb shanks, and pour the stock mixture from the saucepan over everything. 5. Add the wine and rosemary to the crock pot. 6. Cover and cook on low for 8 to 9 hours, or until the lamb is very tender, and serve.

Melt-in-Your-Mouth Sausages

Prep time: 5 minutes | Cook time: 6 to 8 hours | Serves 6 to 8

- 2 pounds (907 g) sweet Italian sausage, cut into 5-inch lengths
- 1 (48-ounce / 1.4-kg) jar spaghetti sauce
- 1 (6-ounce / 170-g) can tomato paste
- 1 large green pepper, thinly sliced
- 1 large onion, thinly sliced
- 1 tablespoon grated Parmesan cheese
- 1 teaspoon dried parsley, or 1 tablespoon chopped fresh parsley
- 1 cup water

1. Place sausage in skillet. Cover with water. Simmer 10 minutes. Drain. 2. Combine remaining ingredients in crock pot. Add sausage. 3. Cover. Cook on low 6 hours. 4. Serve.

Ham and Cheese Casserole

Prep time: 30 minutes | Cook time: 2 to 4 hours | Serves 8 to 10

- 1 (16-ounce / 454-g) package medium egg noodles, divided
- 1 (10¾-ounce / 305-g) can condensed cream of celery soup
- 1 pint sour cream
- 2 cups fully cooked ham, cubed, divided
- 2 cups shredded cheese, your choice, divided

1. Prepare noodles according to package instructions. Drain. 2. In a small bowl combine soup and sour cream until smooth. Set aside. 3. In a greased crock pot, layer one-third of the cooked noodles, one-third of the ham, and one-third of the cheese. 4. Top with one-fourth of soup mixture. 5. Repeat steps 3 and 4 twice until all ingredients are used. The final layer should be the soup-sour cream mixture. 6. Cook 2 to 4 hours on low, or until heated through.

Beef Broccoli

Prep time: 15 minutes | Cook time: 6 hours | Serves 2

- 12 ounces (340 g) flank steak, sliced thin
- 2 cups broccoli florets
- ½ cup low-sodium beef broth
- 2 tablespoons low-sodium soy sauce
- 2 tablespoons honey or maple syrup
- 1 teaspoon toasted sesame oil
- 1 teaspoon minced garlic
- 1 tablespoon cornstarch

1. Put the flank steak and broccoli into the crock pot. 2. In a measuring cup or small bowl, whisk together the beef broth, soy sauce, honey, sesame oil, garlic, and cornstarch. Pour this mixture over the beef and broccoli. 3. Cover and cook on low for 6 hours.

Lamb Shanks Braised Osso Bucco–Style

Prep time: 30 minutes | Cook time: 6 hours | Serves 6

- 6 meaty lamb shanks (about 1 pound / 454 g each), fat trimmed
- 2 teaspoons salt
- 1 teaspoon freshly ground black pepper
- 2 tablespoons olive oil
- 1 medium onion, finely chopped
- 3 medium carrots, finely chopped
- 3 cloves garlic, minced
- Grated zest of 2 lemons
- Grated zest of 1 orange
- ⅔ cup full-bodied red wine
- 1 (18-ounce / 510-g) can tomato purée
- 1 cup beef broth
- ½ cup chicken broth
- ½ cup finely chopped fresh Italian parsley
- 2 tablespoons unsalted butter, at room temperature
- 2 tablespoons all-purpose flour

1. Sprinkle the lamb shanks evenly with the salt and pepper. Heat the oil in a large skillet over high heat. Add as many lamb shanks as will fit in a single layer and brown on all sides. Transfer the browned shanks to the insert of a 5- to 7-quart crock pot. Brown any remaining shanks and transfer them to crock pot insert. 2. Add the onion, carrots, garlic, and citrus zests to the same skillet and sauté until the onion begins to soften. Add the wine and heat, scraping up any browned bits from the bottom of the pan. 3. Transfer the contents of the skillet to the crock pot insert. Stir in the tomato purée and both broths. Cover and cook for 6 hours on low. Remove the shanks from the cooker and cover with aluminum foil to keep warm. Pour the sauce into a saucepan and boil for 10 to 15 minutes, until the sauce has reduced a bit. Add the parsley to the sauce. 4. Mix the butter and flour until smooth in a small bowl and whisk, a bit at a time, into the sauce, bringing it back to a boil after each addition. Taste and adjust the seasoning. 5. Return the sauce and the shanks to the crock pot and keep warm until ready to serve.

Verenike Casserole

Prep time: 15 minutes | Cook time: 5 to 6 hours | Serves 8 to 10

- 24 ounces (680 g) cottage cheese
- 3 eggs
- 1 teaspoon salt
- ½ teaspoon pepper
- 1 cup sour cream
- 2 cups evaporated milk
- 2 cups cubed cooked ham
- 7 to 9 dry lasagna noodles

1. Combine all ingredients except noodles. 2. Place half of creamy ham mixture in bottom of cooker. Add uncooked noodles. Cover with remaining half of creamy ham sauce. Be sure noodles are fully submerged in sauce. 3. Cover. Cook on low 5 to 6 hours. 4. Serve.

Creamy Sausage and Potatoes

Prep time: 15 minutes | Cook time: 6 to 8 hours | Serves 6

- 3 pounds (1.4 kg) small potatoes, peeled and quartered
- 1 pound (454 g) smoked sausage, cut into ¼-inch slices
- 1 (8-ounce / 227-g)
- package cream cheese, softened
- 1 (10¾-ounce / 305-g) can cream of celery soup
- 1 envelope dry ranch salad dressing mix

1. Place potatoes in crock pot. Add sausage. 2. In a bowl, beat together cream cheese, soup, and salad dressing mix until smooth. Pour over potatoes and sausage. 3. Cover and cook on low 6 to 8 hours, or until the potatoes are tender, stirring halfway through cooking time if you're home. Stir again before serving.

Potluck Beef Barbecue

Prep time: 10 minutes | Cook time: 6½ to 8¾ hours | Serves 16

- 1 (4-pound / 1.8-kg) beef chuck roast
- 1 cup brewed coffee or water
- 1 tablespoon cider or red-wine vinegar
- 1 teaspoon salt
- ½ teaspoon pepper
- 1 (14-ounce / 397-g) bottle ketchup
- 1 (15-ounce / 425-g) can tomato sauce
- 1 cup sweet pickle relish
- 2 tablespoons Worcestershire sauce
- ¼ cup brown sugar

1. Place roast, coffee, vinegar, salt, and pepper in crock pot. 2. Cover. Cook on high 6 to 8 hours, or until meat is very tender. 3. Pour off cooking liquid. Shred meat with two forks. 4. Add remaining ingredients. Stir well. 5. Cover. Cook on high 30 to 45 minutes. Reduce heat to low for serving.

Maple Bourbon Pork Chops

Prep time: 15 minutes | Cook time: 3 to 8 hours | Serves 6

- 2 tablespoons olive oil
- 1½ teaspoons salt
- ½ teaspoon freshly ground black pepper
- 6 (1-inch-thick) pork loin chops
- 2 tablespoons unsalted butter
- 2 medium onions, finely chopped
- ½ cup ketchup
- ½ cup bourbon
- ¼ cup pure maple syrup
- 1 teaspoon Tabasco sauce
- 1 teaspoon dry mustard
- ½ cup beef broth

1. Heat the oil in a large skillet over high heat. Sprinkle the salt and pepper evenly over the pork chops and add to the skillet. 2. Brown the chops on both sides, adding a few at a time, being careful not to crowd the pan, and transfer to the insert of a 5- to 7-quart crock pot. 3. Melt the butter in the skillet over medium-high heat. Add the onions and sauté until they begin to soften, about 5 minutes. Add the remaining ingredients and scrape up any browned bits from the bottom of the pan. Transfer the contents of the skillet to the crock pot insert. 4. Cover and cook on high for 3 to 4 hours or on low for 6 to 8 hours. Skim off any fat from the top of the sauce. 5. Serve from the cooker set on warm.

Rosemary Lamb Chops

Prep time: 15 minutes | Cook time: 6 hours | Serves 4

- 3 tablespoons extra-virgin olive oil, divided
- 1½ pounds (680 g) lamb shoulder chops
- Salt, for seasoning
- Freshly ground black
- pepper, for seasoning
- ½ cup chicken broth
- 1 sweet onion, sliced
- 2 teaspoons minced garlic
- 2 teaspoons dried rosemary
- 1 teaspoon dried thyme

1. Lightly grease the insert of the crock pot with 1 tablespoon of the olive oil. 2. In a large skillet over medium-high heat, heat the remaining 2 tablespoons of the olive oil. 3. Season the lamb with salt and pepper. Add the lamb to the skillet and brown for 6 minutes, turning once. 4. Transfer the lamb to the insert, and add the broth, onion, garlic, rosemary, and thyme. 5. Cover and cook on low for 6 hours. 6. Serve warm.

Cinco de Mayo Pork

Prep time: 15 minutes | Cook time: 4 to 8 hours | Serves 6 to 8

- 2 tablespoons vegetable oil
- 1 teaspoon ground cumin
- ½ teaspoon chili powder
- 2 cloves garlic, minced
- 3 pounds (1.4 kg) boneless pork shoulder meat, excess fat removed, cut into 2-inch pieces
- 2 teaspoons salt
- 1 cup prepared salsa (medium, or hot if you like a bit more heat)
- ½ cup beef broth
- 1 (16-ounce / 454-g) package frozen corn, defrosted
- Flour or corn tortillas for serving

1. Heat the oil in a large skillet over medium heat. Add the cumin, chili powder, and garlic and sauté until the garlic and spices are fragrant, about 1 minute. 2. Sprinkle the meat with the salt and brown the pork on all sides in the seasonings. Transfer the pork to the insert of a 5- to 7-quart crock pot. Add the salsa and broth to the skillet, scraping up any browned bits from the bottom. 3. Transfer the contents of the skillet to the insert and add the corn. Stir to combine. Cook on on high for 4 hours or low for 8 hours, until the meat is tender. Serve the pork with warmed tortillas.

Moroccan Meatballs in Spicy Tomato Sauce

Prep time: 20 minutes | Cook time: 6 hours | Serves 6

- Moroccan Meatballs:
- ½ cup bread crumbs
- ¼ cup dried currants
- ½ yellow onion, finely chopped
- ½ teaspoon sea salt
- ½ teaspoon ground cumin
- ½ teaspoon dried oregano
- ¼ teaspoon ground cinnamon
- 1½ pounds (680 g) lean ground beef
- 1 large egg white
- Spicy Tomato Sauce:
- ¼ cup tomato paste
- 1 teaspoon fennel seeds

- 1 teaspoon orange zest
- ½ teaspoon ground cumin
- ¼ teaspoon ground cinnamon
- ¼ teaspoon sea salt
- ¼ teaspoon ground red pepper
- 1 (28-ounce / 794-g) can whole tomatoes, coarsely chopped, with the juice
- 3 cups hot cooked couscous, for serving
- 2 tablespoons fresh chopped parsley, for serving (optional)

Make the Meatballs: 1. Combine the bread crumbs, currants, onion, salt, cumin, oregano, cinnamon, beef, and egg white in a medium bowl. Shape the meat mixture into 30 meatballs and place on a plate. 2. Heat a large nonstick skillet over medium-high heat. Add half of the meatballs to the pan and cook for 3 minutes or until browned, turning frequently. Place the browned meatballs in the crock pot. Repeat, with the remaining 15 meatballs. Prepare the Sauce: 3. Combine the tomato paste, fennel seeds, orange zest, cumin, cinnamon, salt, red pepper, and tomatoes in a medium bowl. Add to the crock pot and stir gently to coat the meatballs with sauce. 4. Cover and cook on low for 6 hours. 5. Serve over the couscous. Garnish with parsley, if desired.

Szechuan Baby Back Ribs

Prep time: 10 minutes | Cook time: 8 to 10 hours | Serves 6

- 2 teaspoons freshly ground black pepper
- 1 teaspoon kosher salt
- ½ teaspoon ground coriander
- ½ teaspoon garlic powder
- ½ teaspoon ground cumin
- ¼ teaspoon ground ginger
- 3 pounds (1.4 kg) baby back ribs, trimmed

- ½ cup water
- 1 small onion, sliced
- 1 garlic clove, minced
- ½ cup honey
- ½ cup Sriracha
- 2½ tablespoons Asian chili sauce (such as sambal oelek)
- ¼ cup brown sugar

1. In a small bowl, mix together the pepper, salt, coriander, garlic powder, cumin, and ginger. Rub the mix on the ribs. Add the water to the crock pot, followed by the ribs. Top the

meat with the onion and garlic. Cover and cook on low for 8 to 10 hours. 2. Preheat your oven's broiler. In another small bowl, make the glaze by combining the honey, Sriracha, chili sauce, and brown sugar. Gently remove the ribs from the liquid and transfer to an aluminum foil–lined baking sheet. Discard the cooking liquid, onion, and garlic. Generously brush the ribs with the glaze and broil them, watching closely to avoid burning, until caramelized, 3 to 5 minutes. Remove them from the oven and enjoy immediately.

Coca-Cola Ham

Prep time: 10 minutes | Cook time: 8 to 10 hours | Serves 6 to 8

- ½ cup Coca-Cola
- 1 cup firmly packed light brown sugar
- ¼ cup dark rum
- 2 tablespoons fresh lime

- juice
- Grated zest of 1 lime
- 1 (5-pound / 2.3-kg) smoked ham

1. Mix the cola, sugar, rum, and lime juice and zest in the insert of a 5- to 7-quart crock pot. Set the ham on top of the mixture and spoon some of the glaze over the top. Cover and cook on low for 8 to 10 hours, spooning glaze over the ham a few times as it cooks. 2. Remove the ham from the crock pot insert, cover with aluminum foil, and allow it to rest for 15 minutes. If you would like to reduce the glaze, spoon off any fat from the top and pour the glaze into a saucepan. Bring to a boil and continue to boil, stirring frequently, until reduced to about 2 cups. (You will have a lot of liquid from the ham that has diluted the glaze.) 3. Slice the ham and spoon the glaze over the slices.

Crock pot Chili

Prep time: 25 minutes | Cook time: 6 to 12 hours | Serves 8 to 10

- 3 pounds (1.4 kg) beef stewing meat, browned
- 2 cloves garlic, minced
- ¼ teaspoon pepper
- ½ teaspoon cumin
- ¼ teaspoon dry mustard
- 1 (7½-ounce / 213-g) can jalapeño relish
- 1 cup beef broth
- 1 to 1½ onions, chopped, according to your taste preference
- ½ teaspoon salt
- ½ teaspoon dried oregano

- 1 tablespoon chili powder
- 1 (7-ounce / 198-g) can green chilies, chopped
- 1 (14½-ounce / 411-g) can stewed tomatoes, chopped
- 1 (15-ounce / 425-g) can tomato sauce
- 2 (15-ounce / 425-g) cans red kidney beans, rinsed and drained
- 2 (15-ounce / 425-g) cans pinto beans, rinsed and drained

1. Combine all ingredients except kidney and pinto beans in crock pot. 2. Cover. Cook on low 10 to 12 hours, or on high 6 to 7 hours. Add beans halfway through cooking time. 3. Serve.

Pork Loin Braised in Cider with Apples and Cream

Prep time: 20 minutes | Cook time: 4 hours | Serves 6 to 8

- 2 tablespoons olive oil
- ½ cup Dijon mustard
- ½ cup firmly packed light brown sugar
- 1 (2½- to 3-pound / 1.1- to 1.4-kg) pork loin roast, rolled and tied
- 1 large onion, finely sliced
- 2 teaspoons dried thyme
- ½ cup apple cider
- 1 cup beef stock
- 4 large Gala or Braeburn apples, peeled, cored, and cut into 8 wedges each
- ¾ cup heavy cream
- Salt and freshly ground black pepper
- 1 pound (454 g) buttered cooked wide egg noodles

1. Heat the oil in a large sauté pan over medium-high heat. Make a paste of the mustard and sugar and spread over the roast on all sides. Add the roast to the pan and brown on all sides. Add the onion and thyme to the sauté pan and cook until the onion is softened, 3 to 5 minutes. 2. Transfer the roast, onion, and any bits from the bottom of the pan to the insert of a 5- to 7-quart crock pot. Add the cider and beef stock. Cover the crock pot and cook on high for 3 hours. Remove the cover and add the apples and cream. Cover and cook on high for an additional 1 hour. 3. Remove the pork from the crock pot insert, cover with aluminum foil, and allow to rest for 15 minutes. Season the sauce with salt and pepper. Remove the strings from the roast, cut into thin slices, and serve the pork on the buttered noodles, napping both with some of the sauce.

Pork Loin in Plum Bourbon Sauce

Prep time: 20 minutes | Cook time: 4 to 10 hours | Serves 8

- 24 dried plums
- 1½ cups beef broth
- 1 (4-pound / 1.8-kg) pork loin roast, rolled and tied
- ½ cup Dijon mustard
- ⅔ cup firmly packed dark brown sugar
- 1 tablespoon vegetable oil
- ⅓ cup bourbon
- 1 teaspoon dried sage
- 1½ teaspoons dried thyme
- 1 tablespoon cornstarch mixed with 2 tablespoons water
- ¼ cup chopped fresh Italian parsley

1. Combine the plums and beef broth in the insert of a 5- to 7-quart crock pot. Dry the outside of the roast with paper towels. Rub the meat all over with the mustard, then roll it in the brown sugar, coating it evenly. 2. Heat the oil in a large skillet over medium-high heat. Add the roast and brown on all sides, making sure the sugar doesn't burn. Transfer the pork to the crock pot insert. Add the bourbon, sage, and thyme to the skillet and scrape up any browned bits from the bottom of the pan. Transfer to the crock pot insert. Cover and cook on high for 4 to 5 hours or on low for 8 to 10 hours. Transfer the pork

and plums to a serving platter. Cover with aluminum foil, and allow the roast to rest for 20 minutes. 3. Strain the cooking liquid through a fine-mesh sieve into a saucepan and skim off as much fat as possible from the top of the sauce. Bring to a boil and taste and adjust the seasonings. Stir in the cornstarch mixture and bring to a boil, stirring constantly. Reduce the heat to medium and stir in the parsley. 4. Cut the strings on the meat and cut into ½-inch-thick slices. Serve the pork and plums with the sauce on the side.

Apple and Onion Beef Pot Roast

Prep time: 20 minutes | Cook time: 5 to 6 hours | Serves 8 to 10

- 1 (3-pound / 1.4-kg) boneless beef roast, cut in half
- Oil
- 1 cup water
- 1 teaspoon seasoned salt
- ½ teaspoon soy sauce
- ½ teaspoon Worcestershire sauce
- ¼ teaspoon garlic powder
- 1 large tart apple, quartered
- 1 large onion, sliced
- 2 tablespoons cornstarch
- 2 tablespoons water

1. Brown roast on all sides in oil in skillet. Transfer to crock pot. 2. Add water to skillet to loosen browned bits. Pour over roast. 3. Sprinkle with seasoned salt, soy sauce, Worcestershire sauce, and garlic powder. 4. Top with apple and onion. 5. Cover. Cook on low 5 to 6 hours. 6. Remove roast and onion. Discard apple. Let stand 15 minutes. 7. To make gravy, pour juices from roast into saucepan and simmer until reduced to 2 cups. Combine cornstarch and water until smooth in small bowl. Stir into beef broth. Bring to boil. Cook and stir for 2 minutes until thickened. 8. Slice pot roast and serve with gravy.

Magic Meat Loaf

Prep time: 20 minutes | Cook time: 9 to 11 hours | Serves 6

- 1 egg, beaten
- ¼ cup milk
- 1½ teaspoons salt
- 2 slices bread, crumbled
- 1½ pounds (680 g) ground beef
- Half a small onion, chopped
- 2 tablespoons chopped
- green peppers
- 2 tablespoons chopped celery
- Ketchup
- Green pepper rings
- 4 to 6 potatoes, cubed
- 3 tablespoons butter, melted

1. Combine egg, milk, salt, and bread crumbs in large bowl. 2. Allow bread crumbs to soften. Add meat, onions, green peppers, and celery. Shape into loaf and place off to the side in crock pot. 3. Top with ketchup and green pepper rings. 4. Toss potatoes with melted butter. Spoon into cooker alongside meat loaf. 5. Cover. Cook on high 1 hour, then on low 8 to 10 hours.

Sausage-Sauerkraut Supper

Prep time: 20 minutes | Cook time: 8 to 9 hours | Serves 10 to 12

- 4 cups cubed carrots
- 4 cups cubed red potatoes
- 2 (14-ounce / 397-g) cans sauerkraut, rinsed and drained
- 2½ pounds (1.1 kg) fresh Polish sausage, cut into 3-inch pieces
- 1 medium onion, thinly sliced
- 3 garlic cloves, minced
- 1½ cups dry white wine or chicken broth
- ½ teaspoon pepper
- 1 teaspoon caraway seeds

1. Layer carrots, potatoes, and sauerkraut in crock pot. 2. Brown sausage in skillet. Transfer to crock pot. Reserve 1 tablespoon drippings in skillet. 3. Sauté onion and garlic in drippings until tender. Stir in wine. Bring to boil. Stir to loosen brown bits. Stir in pepper and caraway seeds. Pour over sausage. 4. Cover. Cook on low 8 to 9 hours.

Braised Tamarind Pork Ribs

Prep time: 20 minutes | Cook time: 6 to 8 hours | Serves 6 to 8

- ⅓ cup tamarind pulp
- 2¾ cups boiling water
- 8 garlic cloves, minced
- 1½-inch piece fresh ginger, grated
- ⅓ cup soy sauce
- 2 teaspoons coriander seeds, ground
- 2 star anise
- 1 teaspoon fennel seeds
- 2 fresh green chiles, finely chopped
- ⅓ cup dark-brown sugar
- 2 racks of pork ribs, 1¾ to 2 pounds (794 to 907 g)

1. Place the tamarind pulp in a bowl and add the boiling water. Let it soak for 15 minutes, and then mash it up using a fork. Strain the tamarind water into a large bowl and discard all the solids. 2. Preheat the crock pot on high. Pour in the tamarind liquid, garlic, ginger, soy sauce, ground coriander seeds, anise, fennel seeds, chopped chiles, and brown sugar. Stir until all of the sugar dissolves. 3. Using a sharp knife, scrape the underside of the ribs on one end, and you will see a transparent membrane. Pull this membrane (use a cloth for a better grip) from the back of the ribs to remove it. If the full rack doesn't fit into the cooker, cut it into smaller racks. 4. Put the ribs into the cooker and make sure they are submerged in the marinade. Cover and cook on low for 8 hours, or on high for 6 hours. 5. When cooked, remove the ribs and either cover them in foil to keep warm, or finish them in the oven for 20 minutes at 350ºF (180ºC) to crisp them up. 6. Turn the crock pot to high, remove the cover, and reduce the sauce to thicken, about 5 minutes. Push through a sieve and use as a dipping sauce or drizzle over the cooked ribs.

Turkey-Beef Loaf

Prep time: 10 minutes | Cook time: 4 to 10 hours | Serves 8

- ½ pound (227 g) extra-lean ground beef
- 1 pound (454 g) lean ground turkey
- 1 medium onion, chopped
- 2 eggs
- ⅔ cup dry quick oats
- 1 envelope dry onion soup mix
- ½ to 1 teaspoon liquid smoke
- 1 teaspoon dry mustard
- 1 cup ketchup, divided
- Nonfat cooking spray

1. Mix beef, turkey, and chopped onion thoroughly. 2. Combine with eggs, oats, dry soup mix, liquid smoke, mustard, and all but 2 tablespoons of ketchup. 3. Shape into loaf and place in crock pot sprayed with nonfat cooking spray. Top with remaining ketchup. 4. Cover. Cook on low 8 to 10 hours, or on high 4 to 6 hours.

Corned Beef Dinner

Prep time: 10 minutes | Cook time: 10 to 11 hours | Serves 6

- 2 onions, sliced
- 2 garlic cloves, minced
- 3 potatoes, pared and quartered
- 3 carrots, sliced
- 2 bay leaves
- 1 small head cabbage, cut into 4 wedges
- 1 (3- to 4-pound / 1.4- to 1.8-kg) corned beef brisket
- 1 cup water
- ½ cup brown sugar
- 1 tablespoon prepared mustard
- Dash of ground cloves

1. Layer onions, garlic, potatoes, carrots, bay leaves, and cabbage in crock pot. 2. Place brisket on top. 3. Add water. 4. Cover. Cook on low 10 to 11 hours. 5. During last hour of cooking, combine brown sugar, mustard, and cloves. Spread over beef. 6. Discard bay leaves. Slice meat and arrange on platter of vegetables.

Barbecued Hot Dogs

Prep time: 5 minutes | Cook time: 4½ hours | Serves 8

- 1 cup apricot preserves
- 4 ounces (113 g) tomato sauce
- ⅓ cup vinegar
- 2 tablespoons soy sauce
- 2 tablespoons honey
- 1 tablespoon oil
- 1 teaspoon salt
- ¼ teaspoon ground ginger
- 2 pounds (907 g) hot dogs, cut into 1-inch pieces

1. Combine all ingredients except hot dogs in crock pot. 2. Cover. Cook on high 30 minutes. Add hot dog pieces. Cook on low 4 hours. 3. Serve as an appetizer.

Ham with Sweet Potatoes and Oranges

Prep time: 15 minutes | Cook time: 7 to 8 hours | Serves 4

- 2 to 3 sweet potatoes, peeled and sliced ¼-inch thick
- 1 large ham slice
- 3 seedless oranges, peeled and sliced
- 3 tablespoons orange juice concentrate
- 3 tablespoons honey
- ½ cup brown sugar
- 2 tablespoons cornstarch

1. Place sweet potatoes in crock pot. 2. Arrange ham and orange slices on top. 3. Combine remaining ingredients. Drizzle over ham and oranges. 4. Cover. Cook on low 7 to 8 hours. 5. Serve. frozen meatballs. 3. Cover. Cook on high 4 to 6 hours.

Chili Bake

Prep time: 15 minutes | Cook time: 4 to 5 hours | Serves 6

- 3 turkey bacon slices
- ½ pound (227 g) extra-lean ground round beef
- 1 (15½-ounce / 439-g) can lima beans, undrained
- 1 (15-ounce / 425-g) can pork and beans, undrained
- 1 (15-ounce / 425-g) can red kidney beans, drained
- ½ cup ketchup
- ½ cup barbecue sauce
- ¼ cup firmly packed brown sugar
- 1 teaspoon dry mustard

1. Brown bacon until crisp in nonstick skillet. Crumble and set aside. 2. Cook beef in nonstick skillet over medium heat until beef is brown, stirring to crumble beef. 3. Combine all ingredients in crock pot. Stir well. 4. Cover and cook on high for 1 hour; then reduce to low and cook for 3 to 4 hours.

Meal-in-One

Prep time: 25 minutes | Cook time: 4 hours | Serves 6 to 8

- 2 pounds (907 g) ground beef
- 1 onion, diced
- 1 green bell pepper, diced
- 1 teaspoon salt
- ¼ teaspoon pepper
- 1 large bag frozen hash
- brown potatoes
- 1 (16-ounce / 454-g) container sour cream
- 1 (24-ounce / 680-g) container cottage cheese
- 1 cup Monterey Jack cheese, shredded

1. Brown ground beef, onion, and green pepper in skillet. Drain. Season with salt and pepper. 2. In crock pot, layer one-third of the potatoes, meat, sour cream, and cottage cheese. Repeat twice. 3. Cover. Cook on low 4 hours, sprinkling Monterey Jack cheese over top during last hour. 4. Serve.

Sweet and Sour Ribs

Prep time: 15 minutes | Cook time: 8 to 10 hours | Serves 8 to 10

- 3 to 4 pounds (1.4 to 1.8 kg) boneless country-style pork ribs
- 1 (20-ounce / 567-g) pineapple tidbits
- 2 (8-ounce / 227-g) cans tomato sauce
- ½ cup thinly sliced onions
- ½ cup thinly sliced green
- peppers
- ½ cup packed brown sugar
- ¼ cup cider vinegar
- ¼ cup tomato paste
- 2 tablespoons Worcestershire sauce
- 1 garlic clove, minced
- 1 teaspoon salt
- ½ teaspoon pepper

1. Place ribs in crock pot. 2. Combine remaining ingredients. Pour over ribs. 3. Cook on low 8 to 10 hours. 4. Serve.

Balsamic Roast Beef

Prep time: 15 minutes | Cook time: 7 to 8 hours | Serves 8

- 3 tablespoons of extra-virgin olive oil, divided
- 2 pounds (907 g) boneless beef chuck roast
- 1 cup beef broth
- ½ cup balsamic vinegar
- 1 tablespoon minced garlic
- 1 tablespoon granulated erythritol
- ½ teaspoon red pepper flakes
- 1 tablespoon chopped fresh thyme

1. Lightly grease the insert of the crock pot with 1 tablespoon of the olive oil. 2. In a large skillet over medium-high heat, heat the remaining 2 tablespoons of the olive oil. Add the beef and brown on all sides, about 7 minutes total. Transfer to the insert. 3. In a small bowl, whisk together the broth, balsamic vinegar, garlic, erythritol, red pepper flakes, and thyme until blended. 4. Pour the sauce over the beef. 5. Cover and cook on low for 7 to 8 hours. 6. Serve warm.

Barbecued Pot Roast

Prep time: 5 minutes | Cook time: 5 to 6 hours | Serves 10

- 1 (5-pound / 2.3-kg) roast
- 1 (16-ounce / 454-g) bottle honey barbecue sauce
- 1 small onion, chopped
- 1 clove garlic, minced
- Black pepper (optional)
- Montreal seasoning (optional)

1. Place roast in crock pot. 2. Pour barbecue sauce over top. 3. Sprinkle onion over roast, and garlic beside the roast. 4. If you wish, sprinkle with pepper and/or Montreal seasoning. 5. Cover and cook on low 5 to 6 hours. 6. Remove roast from cooker and allow to rest for 10 minutes. Slice and serve with cooking juices.

Holiday Meatballs

Prep time: 10 minutes | Cook time: 3 to 6 hours | Serves 15

- 2 (15-ounce / 425-g) bottles hot ketchup
- 2 cups blackberry wine
- 2 (12-ounce / 340-g) jars apple jelly
- 2 pounds (907 g) frozen, precooked meatballs, or your own favorite meatballs, cooked

1. Heat ketchup, wine, and jelly in crock pot on high. 2. Add

Easy Meat Loaf

Prep time: 5 minutes | Cook time: 2 hours | Serves 5 to 6

- 2 pounds (907 g) ground beef
- 1 (6¼-ounce / 177-g) package stuffing mix for beef, plus seasoning
- 2 eggs, beaten
- ½ cup ketchup, divided

1. Mix beef, dry stuffing, eggs, and ¼ cup ketchup. 2. Shape into an oval loaf. Place in crock pot. Pour remaining ketchup over top. 3. Cover and cook on high for 2 hours.

Chapter ④

Poultry

Chicken and Shrimp Casserole

Prep time: 20 minutes | Cook time: 3 to 8 hours | Serves 6

- 1¼ cups rice, uncooked
- 2 tablespoons butter, melted
- 3 cups fat-free, low-sodium chicken broth
- 1 cup water
- 3 cups cut-up, cooked skinless chicken breast
- 2 (4-ounce / 113-g) cans
- sliced mushrooms, drained
- ⅓ cup light soy sauce
- 1 (12-ounce / 340-g) package shelled frozen shrimp
- 8 green onions, chopped, 2 tablespoons reserved
- ⅔ cup slivered almonds

1. Combine rice and butter in crock pot. Stir to coat rice well. 2. Add remaining ingredients except almonds and 2 tablespoons green onions. 3. Cover. Cook on low 6 to 8 hours, or on high 3 to 4 hours, until rice is tender. 4. Sprinkle almonds and green onions over top before serving.

Sausage Pasta

Prep time: 20 minutes | Cook time: 8 to 10 hours | Serves 6

- 1 pound (454 g) turkey sausage, cut in 1-inch chunks
- 1 cup chopped green and/or red bell peppers
- 1 cup chopped celery
- 1 cup chopped red onions
- 1 cup chopped green zucchini
- 1 (8-ounce / 227-g) can
- tomato paste
- 2 cups water
- 1 (14-ounce / 397-g) tomatoes, chopped
- ¼ cup cooking wine
- 1 tablespoon Italian seasoning
- 1 pound (454 g) pasta, cooked

1. Combine all ingredients except pasta in crock pot. 2. Cover. Cook on low 8 to 10 hours. 3. Add pasta 10 minutes before serving.

Frank's Hot-Sauce Buffalo Wings

Prep time: 15 minutes | Cook time: 3 hours | Serves 8

- 3 pounds (1.4 kg) chicken wing drumettes
- ¼ cup olive oil
- 1½ teaspoons salt
- 1 teaspoon sweet paprika
- Freshly ground black
- pepper
- Sauce:
- 1 cup (2 sticks) unsalted butter, melted
- ½ cup Frank's Red Hot Hot Cayenne Pepper Sauce

1. Coat the insert of a 5- to 7-quart crock pot with nonstick cooking spray. Turn the broiler on and preheat for 10 minutes. 2. Put the wings, olive oil, salt, paprika, and a generous grinding of pepper in a large mixing bowl and toss until the wings are evenly coated. Arrange the wings on a wire rack in a baking sheet and broil until the wings are crispy on one side, about 5 minutes. 3. Turn the wings, and broil until crispy and browned, an additional 5 minutes. 4. Remove from the wings from the oven. If you would like to do this step ahead of time, cool the wings and refrigerate for up to 2 days. Otherwise, put the wings in the prepared cooker insert. 5. Combine the butter and hot sauce in a mixing bowl and stir. Pour the sauce over the wings and turn to coat. 6. Cover and cook on high for 3 hours, turning the wings several times to coat in the sauce. 7. Serve from the cooker set on warm.

Duck Carnitas Tacos

Prep time: 15 minutes | Cook time: 6 hours | Serves 6 to 8

- ½ cup fresh tangerine juice (or orange juice)
- 2 tablespoons fresh lime juice, plus lime wedges for serving
- 2 chipotle chiles in adobo sauce, finely chopped
- 2 garlic cloves, minced
- 1½ teaspoons coarse salt
- 6 duck legs
- Warm tortillas, chopped avocado, chopped radishes, toasted pepitas, and cilantro, for serving

1. Preheat a 5- to 6-quart crock pot. 2. Place tangerine juice, lime juice, chipotles, garlic, and salt in the crock pot, and stir until combined. Add duck, skin side up; cover, and cook on low until tender, 6 hours (or on high for 3 hours). 3. Transfer duck to a platter and let cool slightly. Remove skin; pull meat from bones in large pieces. Pour juices into a heatproof bowl; skim off fat into a separate bowl. 4. In a large nonstick skillet, heat ¼ cup reserved duck fat on high. Add duck and cook, stirring, until crisp, 6 to 7 minutes. Stir a few tablespoons of reserved juices into skillet. Serve immediately with tortillas, avocado, radishes, pepitas, and cilantro.

Thai Chicken

Prep time: 5 minutes | Cook time: 8 to 9 hours | Serves 6

- 6 skinless chicken thighs
- ¾ cup salsa, your choice of heat
- ¼ cup chunky peanut butter
- 1 tablespoon low-sodium soy sauce
- 2 tablespoons lime juice
- 1 teaspoon grated ginger root (optional)
- 2 tablespoons chopped cilantro (optional)
- 1 tablespoon chopped dry-roasted peanuts (optional)

1. Put chicken in crock pot. 2. In a bowl, mix remaining ingredients together, except cilantro and chopped peanuts. 3. Cover and cook on low 8 to 9 hours, or until chicken is cooked through but not dry. 4. Skim off any fat. Remove chicken to a platter and serve topped with sauce. Sprinkle with peanuts and cilantro, if you wish. 5. Serve.

Szechwan-Style Chicken and Broccoli

Prep time: 20 minutes | Cook time: 1 to 3 hours | Serves 4

- 2 whole boneless, skinless chicken or turkey breasts
- Oil
- ½ cup picante sauce
- 2 tablespoons soy sauce
- ½ teaspoon sugar
- ½ tablespoon quick-
- cooking tapioca
- 1 medium onion, chopped
- 2 garlic cloves, minced
- ½ teaspoon ground ginger
- 2 cups broccoli florets
- 1 medium red pepper, cut into pieces

1. Cut chicken into 1-inch cubes and brown lightly in oil in skillet. Place in crock pot. 2. Stir in remaining ingredients. 3. Cover. Cook on high 1 to 1½ hours, or on low 2 to 3 hours.

Herb-Infused Turkey Breast

Prep time: 25 minutes | Cook time: 7 to 8 hours | Serves 6

- 3 tablespoons extra-virgin olive oil, divided
- 1½ pounds (680 g) boneless turkey breasts
- Salt, for seasoning
- Freshly ground black pepper, for seasoning
- 1 cup coconut milk
- 2 teaspoons minced garlic
- 2 teaspoons dried thyme
- 1 teaspoon dried oregano
- 1 avocado, peeled, pitted, and chopped
- 1 tomato, diced
- ½ jalapeño pepper, diced
- 1 tablespoon chopped cilantro

1. Lightly grease the insert of the crock pot with 1 tablespoon of the olive oil. 2. In a large skillet over medium-high heat, heat the remaining 2 tablespoons of the olive oil. 3. Lightly season the turkey with salt and pepper. Add the turkey to the skillet and brown for about 7 minutes, turning once. 4. Transfer the turkey to the insert and add the coconut milk, garlic, thyme, and oregano. 5. Cover and cook on low for 7 to 8 hours. 6. In a small bowl, stir together the avocado, tomato, jalapeño pepper, and cilantro. 7. Serve the turkey topped with the avocado salsa.

Chicken Alfredo

Prep time: 20 minutes | Cook time: 8 hours | Serves 4 to 6

- 1 (16-ounce / 454-g) jar Alfredo sauce
- 4 to 6 boneless, skinless chicken breast halves
- 8 ounces (227 g) dry noodles, cooked
- 1 (4-ounce / 113-g) can mushroom pieces and stems, drained
- 1 cup shredded Mozzarella cheese, or ½ cup grated Parmesan cheese

1. Pour about one-third of Alfredo sauce in bottom of crock pot. 2. Add chicken and cover with remaining sauce. 3. Cover.

Cook on low 8 hours. 4. Fifteen minutes before serving, add noodles and mushrooms, mixing well. Sprinkle top with cheese. Dish is ready to serve when cheese is melted. 5. Serve.

Chicken Sweet and Sour

Prep time: 10 minutes | Cook time: 6½ hours | Serves 8

- 4 medium potatoes, sliced
- 8 boneless, skinless chicken breast halves
- 2 tablespoons cider vinegar
- ¼ teaspoon ground nutmeg
- 1 teaspoon dry basil, or 1 tablespoon chopped fresh basil
- 2 tablespoons brown sugar
- 1 cup orange juice
- Dried parsley flakes
- 1 (17-ounce / 482-g) can water-packed sliced peaches, drained
- Fresh parsley
- Fresh orange slices

1. Place potatoes in greased crock pot. Arrange chicken on top. 2. In separate bowl, combine vinegar, nutmeg, basil, brown sugar, and orange juice. Pour over chicken. Sprinkle with parsley. 3. Cover. Cook on low 6 hours. 4. Remove chicken and potatoes from sauce and arrange on warm platter. 5. Turn cooker to high. Add peaches. When warm, spoon peaches and sauce over chicken and potatoes. Garnish with fresh parsley and orange slices.

Asian Meatballs

Prep time: 30 minutes | Cook time: 3 hours | Makes about 24 meatballs

- Sauce:
- 1 cup soy sauce
- ⅔ cup rice wine (mirin) or dry sherry
- 2 cups chicken broth
- ½ cup white miso
- 1 clove garlic, sliced
- 2 dime-size slices fresh ginger
- Meat Balls:
- 1 pound (454 g) ground turkey
- 1 pound (454 g) lean
- ground pork
- 2 teaspoons freshly grated ginger
- 1 clove garlic, minced
- 4 green onions, finely chopped, plus additional for garnish
- 1 large egg white, beaten
- ½ teaspoon hot sauce
- 2 tablespoons cornstarch mixed with ¼ cup water or chicken broth
- Sesame seeds for garnish

1. Put all the sauce ingredients in the insert of a 5- to 7-quart crock pot and stir to combine. 2. Cover and cook on high while preparing the meatballs. 3. Combine all the meatball ingredients in a large bowl and stir. Roll the mixture into 2-inch balls and place in the crock pot insert. 4. Cover and cook on high for 3 hours, until the meatballs are cooked through and register 175ºF (79ºC) on an instant-read thermometer. 5. Remove the meatballs from the sauce and transfer the sauce to a saucepan. Bring the sauce to a boil, add the cornstarch mixture, and bring back to a boil. 6. Serve the sauce with the meatballs, and garnish with the additional green onions and sesame seeds

Chicken, Corn, and Stuffing

Prep time: 5 minutes | Cook time: 2 to 2½ hours | Serves 4

- 4 boneless, skinless chicken breast halves
- 1 (6-ounce / 170-g) box stuffing mix for chicken
- 1 (16-ounce / 454-g)
- package frozen whole-kernel corn
- Half a stick butter, melted
- 2 cups water

1. Place chicken in bottom of crock pot. 2. Mix remaining ingredients together in a mixing bowl. Spoon over chicken. 3. Cover and cook on high 2 to 2½ hours, or until chicken is tender and the stuffing is dry.

Low-Fat Chicken Cacciatore

Prep time: 15 minutes | Cook time: 8 hours | Serves 10

- 2 pounds (907 g) uncooked boneless, skinless chicken breasts, cubed
- ½ pound (227 g) fresh mushrooms
- 1 bell pepper, chopped
- 1 medium-sized onion, chopped
- 1 (12-ounce / 340-g) can low-sodium chopped
- tomatoes
- 1 (6-ounce / 170-g) can low-sodium tomato paste
- 1 (12-ounce / 340-g) can low-sodium tomato sauce
- ½ teaspoon dried oregano
- ½ teaspoon dried basil
- ½ teaspoon garlic powder
- ½ teaspoon salt
- ½ teaspoon black pepper

1. Combine all ingredients in crock pot. 2. Cover. Cook on low 8 hours. 3. Serve.

Quick-Fried Spicy Chicken

Prep time: 15 minutes | Cook time: 4 to 6 hours | Serves 6

- Chicken:
- 2 tablespoons rapeseed oil
- 4 fresh green chiles, chopped
- 4 garlic cloves, sliced
- 4 tomatoes, chopped
- 1 teaspoon salt
- ½ teaspoon turmeric
- 8 boneless chicken thighs, skinned, trimmed, and cut into chunks
- ¼ cup water
- Quick-Fry:
- 1 tablespoon rapeseed oil
- 1 teaspoon cumin seeds
- 1 red onion, sliced
- 1 red bell pepper, seeded and cut into chunks
- 1 green bell pepper, seeded and cut into chunks
- 2 fresh green chiles, sliced lengthwise
- 1 tomato, chopped
- ½ teaspoon salt
- 1 teaspoon garam masala

Make the Chicken: 1. Heat the crock pot to high and add the oil. 2. Add the chiles, garlic, chopped tomatoes, salt, and turmeric, and cook for a few minutes. Add the chicken pieces and the water. Then stir to coat the chicken. 3. Cover and cook on high for 4 hours, or on low for 6 hours. Make the Quick-Fry: 4. When you are ready to eat, heat the oil in a sauté pan and add the cumin seeds. Cook until fragrant, about 1 minute. 5. Add the onion, red and green pepper chunks, chiles, tomato, salt, and garam masala, and sauté for 5 minutes. 6. Add this pepper mixture to the chicken in the crock pot, cover, and cook on high for another 15 minutes with the cover off, until the peppers are cooked to your taste and the sauce has reduced and thickened.

Chicken and Sausage Cacciatore

Prep time: 35 minutes | Cook time: 8 hours | Serves 4 to 6

- 1 large green pepper, sliced in 1-inch strips
- 1 cup sliced mushrooms
- 1 medium onion, sliced in rings
- 1 pound (454 g) skinless, boneless chicken breasts,
- browned
- 1 pound (454 g) Italian sausage, browned
- ½ teaspoon dried oregano
- ½ teaspoon dried basil
- 1½ cups Italian-style tomato sauce

1. Layer vegetables in crock pot. 2. Top with meat. 3. Sprinkle with oregano and basil. 4. Top with tomato sauce. 5. Cover. Cook on low 8 hours. 6. Remove cover during last 30 minutes of cooking time to allow sauce to cook off and thicken. 7. Serve.

Bistro Chicken Thighs

Prep time: 15 minutes | Cook time: 6 to 8 hours | Serves 6 to 8

- 10 chicken thighs, skin removed
- 1½ teaspoons salt
- ½ teaspoon freshly ground black pepper
- 2 tablespoons extra-virgin olive oil
- 2 tablespoons unsalted butter
- 2 medium onions, coarsely
- chopped
- 3 cloves garlic, minced
- 2 teaspoons dried thyme
- 1 cup red wine
- 1 (14- to 15-ounce / 397- to 425-g) can crushed tomatoes, with their juice
- ½ cup finely chopped fresh Italian parsley

1. Sprinkle the chicken evenly with the salt and pepper. Heat the oil in a large skillet over medium heat. Add the chicken and brown on all sides. 2. Transfer the browned meat to the insert of a 5- to 7-quart crock pot. Melt the butter in the same skillet. Add the onions, garlic, and thyme and sauté until the onion is softened, about 5 minutes. 3. Add the wine and tomatoes and scrape up any browned bits from the bottom of the skillet. Transfer the contents of the pan to the crock pot insert. Cover and cook on low for 6 to 8 hours, until the chicken is cooked through and tender, falling off the bone. Skim off any fat from the top of the sauce. 4. Stir in the parsley and serve from the cooker set on warm.

Chicken Braised in Cider with Apples and Bacon

Prep time: 25 minutes | Cook time: 3 to 4 hours | Serves 8

- 4 tablespoons (½ stick) unsalted butter
- 5 large cooking apples, peeled and cored, cut into 8 wedges each
- 2 medium onions, cut into half rounds
- 2 teaspoons dried thyme
- 2 tablespoons Dijon mustard
- ¼ cup firmly packed light brown sugar
- 1½ cups apple cider
- 2 chicken bouillon cubes
- 8 strips thick-cut Applewood smoked bacon, cut into 1-inch pieces
- 8 chicken breast halves, skin and bones removed
- ½ teaspoon freshly ground black pepper
- ½ cup heavy cream
- ½ cup finely chopped fresh Italian parsley

1. Melt the butter in a large skillet over medium-high heat. Add the apples, onions, and thyme and sauté until the onions begin to soften, 5 to 7 minutes. 2. Add the mustard, sugar, and cider and stir to combine, melting the sugar. Transfer to the insert of a 5- to 7-quart crock pot. Add the bouillon cubes to the cooker, crushing them to dissolve. Set the cooker on warm while you sauté the chicken. 3. Wipe out the skillet, cook the bacon until crisp, and remove it to paper towels to drain. Sprinkle the chicken with the pepper. Add the chicken to the bacon drippings in the skillet and brown on all sides. 4. Transfer the chicken to the crock pot insert. Cover and cook on low for 3 to 4 hours, until the chicken is cooked though and the apples are tender. Add the cream and parsley and stir to combine. 5. Serve from the cooker set on warm.

The Best Thanksgiving Turkey Breast You'll Ever Eat

Prep time: 20 minutes | Cook time: 3½ to 4 hours | Serves 8

- 2 medium onions, quartered
- 2 medium carrots, cut into 1-inch lengths
- 2 stalks celery, cut into 1-inch lengths
- 2 large sprigs thyme leaves
- 1½ teaspoons salt
- ½ teaspoon freshly ground black pepper
- 1 cup double-strength chicken broth
- 4 strips thick-cut bacon
- 1 (3- to 4-pound / 1.4- to 1.8-kg) bone-in turkey breast
- 2 teaspoons Wondra or other instant blending flour (optional)

1. Arrange the vegetables and thyme in the insert of a 5- to 7-quart crock pot. Sprinkle with the salt and pepper and pour in the broth. 2. Arrange the bacon on top of the turkey breast and place in the crock pot insert on top of the vegetables. Cover and cook on high for 3½ to 4 hours, until the turkey registers 170°F (77°C) on an instant-read thermometer. Carefully transfer the turkey breast to a serving platter and discard the bacon. 3. Cover the turkey breast with aluminum foil and allow to rest for 15 minutes. Strain the sauce through a fine-mesh sieve into a saucepan and bring to a boil. Whisk in the flour (if using) and bring back to a boil. Taste and adjust the seasoning. slice the turkey breast and serve with the gravy.

Sausage, Fennel and Chicken

Prep time: 10 minutes | Cook time: 8 hours | Serves 2

- ½ fennel bulb, cored and sliced thin
- ½ red onion, halved and sliced thin
- 1 teaspoon extra-virgin olive oil
- 2 bone-in, skinless chicken thighs, about 8 ounces (227 g) each
- ⅛ teaspoon sea salt
- 1 hot Italian sausage link, casing removed

1. Put the fennel, onion, and olive oil in the crock pot. Gently stir to combine. 2. Season the chicken with the salt and set it atop the fennel and onion. 3. Crumble the sausage around the chicken. 4. Cover and cook on low for 8 hours.

Curried Chicken with Coconut and Basil

Prep time: 20 minutes | Cook time: 6 to 8 hours | Serves 6 to 8

- 4 tablespoons (½ stick) unsalted butter
- 18 chicken thighs, boned and skinned
- 1 teaspoon garam masala
- 2 medium onions, finely chopped
- 1 teaspoon freshly grated ginger
- 2 cloves garlic, minced
- 1 large Granny Smith
- apple, cored and cut into ½-inch dice
- ¼ cup all-purpose flour
- 2 cups chicken broth
- 1½ teaspoons sweet curry powder
- 1 cup coconut milk
- ¼ cup finely chopped fresh basil
- Steamed rice for serving

1. Melt 2 tablespoons of the butter in a large skillet over high heat. Sprinkle the chicken thighs with the garam masala, add to the skillet in batches, and sauté until browned on all sides. Transfer the browned pieces to the insert of a 5- to 7-quart crock pot. Add the onions, ginger, garlic, and apple to the same skillet and sauté over medium-high heat until the onions begin to soften, about 5 minutes. Transfer the contents of the skillet to the crock pot insert. 2. Melt the remaining 2 tablespoons of butter in the skillet. Add the flour and cook, for 3 minutes, whisking constantly. Gradually whisk in the chicken broth and bring the mixture to a boil. 3. Stir in the curry powder and coconut milk. Transfer the sauce to the insert of a crock pot. Cover and cook on low for 6 to 8 hours, until the chicken is tender. Sprinkle the basil over the curry and stir to blend. 4. Serve over steamed rice.

Chicken Meatballs in Chunky Tomato Sauce

Prep time: 45 minutes | Cook time: 5 to 7 hours | Serves 6 to 8

- Quick Marinara:
- 2 tablespoons extra-virgin olive oil
- 1 medium onion, finely chopped
- 2 cloves garlic, minced
- Pinch red pepper flakes (optional)
- 1 teaspoon dried basil
- 2 (28- to 32-ounce / 794- to 907-g) cans crushed tomatoes, with their juice
- 1½ teaspoons salt
- 1 teaspoon freshly ground black pepper
- ½ cups finely chopped fresh Italian parsley

- Chicken Meatballs:
- ¼ cup milk
- 1 cup fresh bread crumbs
- ½ cup freshly grated Parmesan cheese
- 2 tablespoons finely chopped fresh Italian parsley
- ½ cup finely chopped onion
- 1 clove garlic, minced
- 1½ teaspoons salt
- ½ teaspoon freshly ground black pepper
- 2 pounds (907 g) ground chicken or turkey
- 1 large egg, beaten

1. Heat the oil in a small sauté pan over medium-high heat. Add the onion, garlic, red pepper flakes (if using), and basil and sauté until the onion is softened and begins to turn translucent, about 5 minutes. 2. Transfer the mixture to the insert of a 5- to 7-quart crock pot. Add the tomatoes, salt, pepper, and parsley to the cooker and stir to combine. 3. Cover and cook on low for 2 to 4 hours while making the meatballs. 4. Put the milk and the bread crumbs in a large mixing bowl and stir to combine. Add the remaining ingredients and stir until well combined. 5. Form the mixture into 2-inch balls and transfer them to the crock pot insert. Spoon some of the sauce over the meatballs. 6. Cover and cook on high for 3 hours, until the meatballs are cooked through and register 175°F (79°C) on an instant-read thermometer. Skim off any fat from the top of the sauce. 7. Serve the meatballs from the cooker set on warm.

Braised Chicken with Niçzise Olives

Prep time: 15 minutes | Cook time: 4 to 5 hours | Serves 6

- ½ cup all-purpose flour
- Salt and freshly ground black pepper
- 8 chicken thighs, skin and bones removed
- ¼ cup extra-virgin olive oil
- 4 garlic cloves, sliced

- ¾ cup dry white wine or vermouth
- 1½ cup chicken broth
- 1 cup pitted Niçoise olives
- 1 lemon, cut into ½-inch-thick slices
- 1 bay leaf

1. Combine the flour, ½ teaspoon salt, and ½ teaspoon pepper in a large plastic bag. Add the chicken to the bag and shake to coat. Heat the oil in a large skillet over high heat. 2. Add the chicken and brown on all sides, 7 to 10 minutes. 3. Transfer the browned chicken to the insert of a 5- to 7-quart crock pot. Add the garlic to the same skillet and cook until it is fragrant, about 30 seconds. 4. Add the wine and deglaze the skillet, scraping up any browned bits from the bottom. Transfer the contents of the skillet to the crock pot insert. Add the remaining ingredients and stir to combine. Cover the crock pot and cook on low for 4 to 5 hours, until the chicken is tender. 5. Season with salt and pepper before serving.

Reuben Chicken Casserole

Prep time: 30 minutes | Cook time: 4 hours | Serves 6

- 2 (16-ounce / 454-g) cans sauerkraut, rinsed and drained, divided
- 1 cup Light Russian salad dressing, divided
- 6 boneless, skinless chicken

- breast halves, divided
- 1 tablespoon prepared mustard, divided
- 6 slices Swiss cheese
- Fresh parsley for garnish (optional)

1. Place half the sauerkraut in the crock pot. Drizzle with ⅓ cup dressing. 2. Top with 3 chicken breast halves. Spread half the mustard on top of the chicken. 3. Top with remaining sauerkraut and chicken breasts. Drizzle with another ⅓ cup dressing. (Save the remaining dressing until serving time.) 4. Cover and cook on low for 4 hours, or until the chicken is tender, but not dry or mushy. 5. To serve, place a breast half on each of 6 plates. Divide the sauerkraut over the chicken. Top each with a slice of cheese and a drizzle of the remaining dressing. Garnish with parsley if you wish, just before serving.

Chicken, Broccoli, and Rice Casserole

Prep time: 10 minutes | Cook time: 3 to 7 hours | Serves 8

- 1 cup long-grain rice, uncooked
- 3 cups water
- 2 teaspoons low-sodium chicken bouillon granules
- 1 (10¾-ounce / 305-g) can fat-free, low-sodium cream of chicken soup

- 2 cups chopped, cooked chicken breast
- ¼ teaspoon garlic powder
- 1 teaspoon onion salt
- 1 cup shredded, fat-free Cheddar cheese
- 1 (16-ounce / 454-g) bag frozen broccoli, thawed

1. Combine all ingredients except broccoli in crock pot. 2. One hour before end of cooking time, stir in broccoli. 3. Cook on high for a total of 3 to 4 hours, or on low for a total of 6 to 7 hours.

Chicken Pot Pie

Prep time: 15 minutes | Cook time: 8 hours | Serves 2

- 2 boneless, skinless chicken thighs, diced
- 1 cup diced, peeled Yukon Gold potatoes
- 1 cup frozen peas, thawed
- 1 cup diced onions
- 1 cup diced carrots
- 1 teaspoon fresh thyme
- ⅛ teaspoon sea salt
- Freshly ground black pepper
- 1 tablespoon all-purpose flour
- 1 cup low-sodium chicken broth

1. Put the chicken, potatoes, peas, onions, carrots, and thyme in the crock pot. Season with the salt and a few grinds of the pepper. Sprinkle in the flour and toss to coat the chicken and vegetables. Pour in the chicken broth. 2. Cover and cook on low for 8 hours.

Easy Mushroom Chicken

Prep time: 10 minutes | Cook time: 3 to 8 hours | Serves 4 to 6

- 4 to 6 chicken legs and thighs (joined), skinned
- Salt and pepper to taste
- ½ cup chicken broth or dry white wine
- 1 (10¾-ounce / 305-g) can cream of mushroom or celery soup
- 1 (4-ounce / 113-g) can sliced mushrooms, drained

1. Sprinkle salt and pepper on each piece of chicken. Place chicken in crock pot. 2. In a small bowl, mix broth and soup together. Pour over chicken. 3. Spoon mushrooms over top. 4. Cover and cook on low 6 to 8 hours, or on high 3 to 4 hours, or until chicken is tender but not dry.

Chicken Cacciatore with Porcini and Cremini Mushrooms

Prep time: 15 minutes | Cook time: 4 to 5 hours | Serves 6 to 8

- 4 tablespoons extra-virgin olive oil
- 1 pound (454 g) cremini mushrooms, quartered
- 2 teaspoons salt
- Pinch red pepper flakes
- 1 teaspoon dried oregano
- 3 cloves garlic, minced
- ¼ cup dried porcini mushrooms, crumbled
- ¼ cup red wine
- 1 (28- to 32-ounce / 794- to 907-g) can crushed tomatoes, with their juice
- 10 chicken thighs, skin and bones removed

1. Heat 2 tablespoons of the oil in a large skillet over high heat. Add the mushrooms, 1 teaspoon of the salt, red pepper flakes, oregano, and garlic and sauté until the liquid in the pan has evaporated, about 7 to 10 minutes. 2. Add the porcinis and the wine to a small bowl and allow the porcinis to soften. Add the wine mixture and the tomatoes to the skillet. 3. Transfer the contents of the pan to the insert of a 5- to 7-quart crock pot. 4. Sprinkle the chicken evenly with the remaining 1 teaspoon salt. Heat the remaining 2 tablespoons oil in the same skillet over high heat. Add the chicken to the skillet and brown on all sides, 15 to 20 minutes. 5. Transfer the browned meat to the crock pot insert, submerging it in the sauce. Cover and cook on low for 4 to 5 hours, until the chicken is tender and cooked through. Skim off any fat from the top of the sauce. 6. Serve from the cooker set on warm.

Chicken, Sweet Chicken

Prep time: 15 minutes | Cook time: 5 to 6 hours | Serves 6 to 8

- 2 medium raw sweet potatoes, peeled and cut into ¼-inch thick slices
- 8 boneless, skinless chicken thighs
- 1 (8-ounce / 227-g) jar orange marmalade
- ¼ cup water
- ¼ to ½ teaspoon salt
- ½ teaspoon pepper

1. Place sweet potato slices in crock pot. 2. Rinse and dry chicken pieces. Arrange on top of the potatoes. 3. Spoon marmalade over the chicken and potatoes. 4. Pour water over all. Season with salt and pepper. 5. Cover and cook on high 1 hour, and then turn to low and cook 4 to 5 hours, or until potatoes and chicken are both tender.

Cuban Chicken and Beans

Prep time: 20 minutes | Cook time: 7 hours | Serves 2

- 2 boneless, skinless chicken breasts
- 2 teaspoons jerk seasoning
- ½ teaspoon salt
- 1 onion, chopped
- 2 garlic cloves, minced
- 1 serrano pepper, minced
- 1 (14 ounces / 397 g) can black beans, rinsed and drained
- ⅔ cup long grain brown rice
- 1⅓ cups chicken stock
- 2 tablespoons freshly squeezed lime juice
- 1 tablespoon honey
- 1 bay leaf
- 2 tablespoons minced black olives
- 1 mango, peeled and cubed

1. On a platter, sprinkle the chicken breasts with the jerk seasoning and salt; set aside. 2. In the crock pot, combine the onion, garlic, serrano pepper, black beans, and rice. 3. Pour the stock, lime juice, and honey into the crock pot, and mix. Add the bay leaf. 4. Top with the chicken and sprinkle with the olives. 5. Cover and cook on low for 6 to 7 hours, or until the chicken registers 160ºF (71ºC) on a meat thermometer. 6. Remove the chicken from the crock pot to a clean platter. Remove the bay leaf from the crock pot and discard. 7. Stir the mango into the mixture in the crock pot, and serve with the chicken.

Hot Buffalo Chicken Wings

Prep time: 10 minutes | Cook time: 6 hours | Serves 8

- 1 (12 ounces / 340 g) bottle hot pepper sauce
- ¾ cup melted grass-fed butter
- 1 tablespoon dried oregano
- 2 teaspoons garlic powder
- 1 teaspoon onion powder
- 3 pounds (1.4 kg) chicken wing sections

1. In a large bowl, whisk together the hot sauce, butter, oregano, garlic powder, and onion powder until blended. 2. Add the chicken wings and toss to coat. 3. Pour the mixture into the insert of a crock pot. 4. Cover and cook on low for 6 hours. 5. Serve.

Chicken Chili Verde

Prep time: 20 minutes | Cook time: 8 hours | Serves 6

- 1½ pounds (680 g) boneless, skinless chicken thighs
- 2 pounds (907 g) tomatillos, husked, cleaned, and puréed
- 1 medium onion, finely chopped
- 3 garlic cloves, minced
- ½ cup finely chopped fresh cilantro
- 2½ cups low-sodium chicken stock
- 1 tablespoon chili powder, preferably ancho
- 1 teaspoon ground cumin
- 1 teaspoon kosher salt, plus more for seasoning
- 1 (14½-ounce / 411-g) can cannellini or pinto beans, drained and rinsed
- Freshly ground black pepper
- 1 cup crushed tortilla chips, for garnish
- ½ cup sour cream, for garnish
- 1 medium red onion, finely chopped, for garnish
- 1 lime, cut into wedges, for garnish

1. Put the chicken in the crock pot, along with the puréed tomatillos, onion, garlic, cilantro, chicken stock, chili powder, cumin, salt, and beans. Stir to combine. Cover and cook on low for 8 hours. 2. Use two forks to shred the chicken. Season with additional salt and pepper, as needed. Ladle into the bowls and garnish with the tortilla chips, sour cream, red onion, and a squirt of lime.

Chicken Fajitas

Prep time: 15 minutes | Cook time: 6 hours | Serves 2

- 1 onion, halved and sliced thin
- 3 sweet bell peppers, assorted colors, cored and sliced thin
- ½ teaspoon ground cumin
- ½ teaspoon smoked paprika
- ¼ teaspoon red pepper flakes
- 16 ounces (454 g) boneless, skinless chicken breast, cut into 4-inch-long tenders
- 1 teaspoon extra-virgin olive oil
- ⅛ teaspoon sea salt
- 4 corn tortillas
- ¼ cup fresh cilantro, for garnish
- 1 small avocado, sliced, for garnish
- 1 lime, cut into wedges, for garnish

1. Put the onion, bell peppers, cumin, paprika, red pepper flakes, chicken, and olive oil in the crock pot and toss to combine. Season the chicken and vegetables with the salt. 2. Cover and cook on low for 6 hours. 3. Serve the fajita mixture with warmed corn tortillas and garnished with the cilantro, avocado, and a generous squeeze of fresh lime juice.

Chicken Tinga Tacos

Prep time: 15 minutes | Cook time: 6 hours | Serves 4

- 2 pounds (907 g) boneless, skinless chicken thighs
- 1 teaspoon kosher salt, plus more for seasoning
- 2 ounces (57 g) Mexican chorizo, casing removed
- 2 (14½-ounce / 411-g) can diced, fire-roasted tomatoes, undrained
- 2 cups store-bought salsa
- 2 or 3 chipotle chiles en
- adobo, finely chopped, plus 1 tablespoon adobo sauce
- 1 tablespoon apple cider vinegar
- 10 to 12 tortillas, warm, for serving
- 2 avocados, peeled, pitted, and diced
- ¼ cup chopped red onion
- ¼ cup chopped fresh cilantro

1. Season the chicken with the salt. Put the chicken in the crock pot, along with the chorizo, tomatoes, salsa, chipotle chiles and sauce, and vinegar and stir to combine. Cover and cook on low for 6 hours, until tender. 2. Remove the cover. Use two forks to shred the meat and mix with the sauce to coat. Season with additional salt, as needed. 3. Serve the mixture in the warm tortillas with the avocado, red onion, and cilantro.

Slow-Cooked Turkey Dinner

Prep time: 15 minutes | Cook time: 7½ hours | Serves 4 to 6

- 1 onion, diced
- 6 small red potatoes, quartered
- 2 cups sliced carrots
- 1½ to 2 pounds (680 to 907 g) boneless, skinless turkey thighs
- ¼ cup flour
- 2 tablespoons dry onion soup mix
- 1 (10¾-ounce / 305-g) can cream of mushroom soup
- ⅔ cup chicken broth or water

1. Place vegetables in bottom of crock pot. 2. Place turkey thighs over vegetables. 3. Combine remaining ingredients. Pour over turkey. 4. Cover. Cook on high 30 minutes. Reduce heat to low and cook 7 hours.

Asian Honey Wings

Prep time: 15 minutes | Cook time: 3 hours | Serves 6 to 8

- 3 pounds (1.4 kg) chicken wing drumettes
- ¼ cup olive oil
- 1½ teaspoons salt
- 1 teaspoon sweet paprika
- ½ teaspoon freshly ground black pepper
- Sauce:
- 1 cup honey
- ½ cup soy sauce
- ½ cup hoisin sauce
- ¼ cup rice wine (mirin) or dry sherry
- 2 cloves garlic, minced
- 1 teaspoon freshly grated ginger

1. Coat the insert of a 5- to 7-quart crock pot with nonstick cooking spray. Turn the broiler on and preheat for 10 minutes. 2. Put the wings, olive oil, salt, paprika, and pepper in a large mixing bowl and toss to coat the wings evenly. Arrange the wings on a rack in a baking sheet and broil until the wings are crispy on one side, about 5 minutes. 3. Turn the wings and broil until crispy and browned, another 5 minutes 4. Remove the wings from the oven. If you would like to do this step ahead of time, cool the wings and refrigerate for up to 2 days; otherwise, place the wings in the prepared cooker insert. 5. Combine all the sauce ingredients in a mixing bowl and stir. Pour over the wings and turn to coat. 6. Cover and cook on high for 3 hours, stirring twice during the cooking time to make sure the wings are cooking evenly. 7. Serve from the cooker set on warm.

Smoked-Paprika Chicken Thighs

Prep time: 20 minutes | Cook time: 6 to 8 hours | Serves 6 to 8

- 6 strips thick-cut bacon, cut into 1-inch pieces
- 10 chicken thighs, skin removed
- 1½ teaspoons salt
- ½ teaspoon freshly ground black pepper
- 2 tablespoons olive oil
- 2 medium onions, cut into half rounds
- 2 medium red bell peppers, seeded and cut into ½-inch-thick slices
- 1 medium yellow bell pepper, seeded and cut into
- ½-inch-thick slices
- 1 medium orange bell pepper, seeded and cut into ½-inch-thick slices
- 2 cloves garlic, minced
- 1½ teaspoons smoked paprika
- 1 (14- to 15-ounce / 397- to 425-g) can double-strength chicken broth (not diluted)
- 1 (14- to 15-ounce / 397- to 425-g) can chopped tomatoes, drained
- ½ cup finely chopped fresh Italian parsley

1. Cook the bacon in a large skillet over medium heat until crisp and remove it to paper towels to drain, leaving the drippings in the pan. 2. Sprinkle the chicken evenly with the salt and pepper and add to the bacon drippings. Brown the chicken on all sides, about 7 to 10 minutes. 3. Transfer the browned chicken pieces to the insert of a 5- to 7-quart crock pot. Heat the oil in the same skillet over medium-high heat. Add the onions, bell peppers, and garlic and sauté until the vegetables begin to soften, 4 to 6 minutes. Add the paprika and sauté for 2 minutes. Add the broth and scrape up any browned bits from the bottom of the skillet. 4. Transfer the contents of the skillet to the crock pot insert. Add the tomatoes and stir to combine. Cover and cook on low for 6 to 8 hours, until the chicken is cooked through and tender. Skim off any fat from the top of the sauce. 5. Stir in the reserved bacon and the parsley and serve from the cooker set on warm.

Southern Barbecue Spaghetti Sauce

Prep time: 20 minutes | Cook time: 4 to 5 hours | Serves 12

- 1 pound (454 g) lean ground turkey
- 2 medium onions, chopped
- 1½ cups sliced fresh mushrooms
- 1 medium green bell pepper, chopped
- 2 garlic cloves, minced
- 1 (14½-ounce / 411-g) can diced tomatoes, undrained
- 1 (12-ounce / 340-g) can
- tomato paste
- 1 (8-ounce / 227-g) can tomato sauce
- 1 cup ketchup
- ½ cup fat-free beef broth
- 2 tablespoons Worcestershire sauce
- 2 tablespoons brown sugar
- 1 tablespoon ground cumin
- 2 teaspoons chili powder
- 12 cups spaghetti, cooked

1. In a large nonstick skillet, cook the turkey, onions, mushrooms, green pepper, and garlic over medium heat until meat is no longer pink. Drain. 2. Transfer to crock pot. Stir in tomatoes, tomato paste, tomato sauce, ketchup, broth, Worcestershire sauce, brown sugar, cumin, and chili powder. Mix well. 3. Cook on low 4 to 5 hours. Serve over spaghetti.

Chicken and Vegetables

Prep time: 15 minutes | Cook time: 6 hours | Serves 4

- 1 (2.9-ounce / 82-g) packages dry bearnaise sauce mix
- ½ cup dry white wine
- 1 pound (454 g) boneless, skinless chicken breasts, cut into bite-sized cubes
- 1 (9-ounce / 255-g) package frozen mixed vegetables
- 1 pound (454 g) cooked
- ham, cubed
- 1 pound (454 g) red potatoes, cubed
- 1 red bell pepper, chopped
- 1 green bell pepper, chopped
- 3 shallots, minced
- ½ teaspoon garlic powder
- ½ teaspoon turmeric powder
- ½ teaspoon dried tarragon

1. Combine all ingredients in crock pot. 2. Cover. Cook on low 6 hours.

Chicken Mole

Prep time: 15 minutes | Cook time: 7 to 8 hours | Serves 6

- 3 tablespoons extra-virgin olive oil or ghee, divided
- 2 pounds (907 g) boneless chicken thighs and breasts
- Salt, for seasoning
- Freshly ground black pepper, for seasoning
- 1 sweet onion, chopped
- 1 tablespoon minced garlic
- 1 (28 ounces / 794 g) can diced tomatoes
- 4 dried chile peppers, soaked in water for 2 hours and

chopped
- 3 ounces (85 g) dark chocolate, chopped
- ¼ cup natural peanut butter
- 1½ teaspoons ground cumin
- ¾ teaspoon ground cinnamon
- ½ teaspoon chili powder
- ½ cup coconut cream
- 2 tablespoons chopped cilantro, for garnish

1. Lightly grease the insert of the crock pot with 1 tablespoon of the olive oil. 2. In a large skillet over medium-high heat, heat the remaining 2 tablespoons of the olive oil. 3. Lightly season the chicken with salt and pepper, add to the skillet, and brown for about 5 minutes, turning once. 4. Add the onion and garlic and sauté for an additional 3 minutes. 5. Transfer the chicken, onion, and garlic to the crock pot, and stir in the tomatoes, chiles, chocolate, peanut butter, cumin, cinnamon, and chili powder. 6. Cover and cook on low for 7 to 8 hours. 7. Stir in the coconut cream, and serve hot, topped with the cilantro.

Chicken Curry

Prep time: 30 minutes | Cook time: 4 hours | Serves 8

- 3 pounds (1.4 kg) boneless, skinless chicken thighs
- 2 onions, halved and thinly sliced
- 8 garlic cloves, thinly sliced
- 1 (2-inch) piece peeled fresh ginger, thinly sliced
- 2 tablespoons curry powder, preferably Madras
- 2 teaspoon ground coriander
- 2 teaspoon ground cumin
- 2 teaspoons coarse salt
- 2 cups unsweetened coconut milk
- 2 (10-ounce / 283-g) packages frozen green peas
- Cooked basmati rice, for serving

1. Preheat a 5- to 6-quart crock pot. 2. Place chicken, onions, garlic, ginger, curry powder, coriander, and cumin in the crock pot, and toss to coat. Add salt. Cover and cook on high until chicken is fork-tender, about 4 hours (or on low for 8 hours). 3. Stir in coconut milk and peas. Cover and cook on high until peas are heated through, about 20 minutes (or on low for 40 minutes). 4. Transfer chicken to a bowl. Using two forks, break chicken into pieces. Return chicken to pot and toss with sauce. Serve with rice and desired accompaniments.

Fruited Barbecue Chicken

Prep time: 5 minutes | Cook time: 4 hours | Serves 6 to 8

- 1 (29-ounce / 822-g) can tomato sauce
- 1 (20-ounce / 567-g) unsweetened crushed pineapple, undrained
- 2 tablespoons brown sugar
- 3 tablespoons vinegar
- 1 tablespoon instant minced onion
- 1 teaspoon paprika
- 2 teaspoons Worcestershire sauce
- ¼ teaspoon garlic powder
- ⅛ teaspoon pepper
- 3 pounds (1.4 kg) chicken, skinned and cubed
- 1 (11-ounce / 312-g) can mandarin oranges, drained

1. Combine all ingredients except chicken and oranges. Add chicken pieces. 2. Cover. Cook on high 4 hours. 3. Just before serving, stir in oranges. Serve.

Chapter 5

Fish and Seafood

Halibut with Eggplant and Ginger Relish

Prep time: 25 minutes | Cook time: 4 hours | Serves 4

- 4 medium Japanese eggplants (or 2 large eggplants), cut into ½-inch cubes
- ¼ cup coarse salt
- ¼ cup extra-virgin olive oil
- 2 onions, diced
- 3 garlic cloves, minced
- 1 (1-inch) piece fresh ginger, peeled and finely grated
- 2 kaffir lime leaves
- 2 teaspoon brown sugar
- 1 tablespoon rice vinegar
- ¼ cup fresh lime juice
- 1 cup packed fresh cilantro, finely chopped
- 1 pound (454 g) halibut, cut into 1-inch pieces
- ½ cup unsweetened flaked coconut, toasted, for garnish

1. Combine eggplant and salt in a colander set over a bowl; let stand about 1 hour. Rinse well and pat dry. 2. Preheat a 5- to 6-quart crock pot. 3. Heat 2 tablespoons oil in a large skillet over medium. Add onions and sauté until deeply golden, about 15 minutes. Add garlic and ginger, and cook 2 more minutes. Add eggplants and cook just until hot. Transfer vegetables to the crock pot. 4. Add remaining 2 tablespoons oil, the lime leaves, brown sugar, vinegar, and lime juice to crock pot. Cover and cook on low until very soft but not mushy, about 4 hours (or on high for 2 hours). 5. Stir in cilantro. Nestle fish on top of eggplant mixture and cook on low until cooked through, about 20 minutes (or on high for 10 minutes). Serve relish topped with halibut and sprinkled with toasted coconut.

Spicy Tomato Basil Mussels

Prep time: 15 minutes | Cook time: 7 hours | Serves 4

- 3 tablespoons olive oil
- 4 cloves garlic, minced
- 3 shallot cloves, minced
- 8 ounces (227 g) mushrooms, diced
- 1 (28-ounce / 794-g) can diced tomatoes, with the juice
- ¾ cup white wine
- 2 tablespoons dried oregano
- ½ tablespoon dried basil
- ½ teaspoon black pepper
- 1 teaspoon paprika
- ¼ teaspoon red pepper flakes
- 3 pounds (1.4 kg) mussels

1. In a large sauté pan, heat the olive oil over medium-high heat. Cook the garlic, shallots, and mushrooms for 2 to 3 minutes, until the garlic is just a bit brown and fragrant. Scrape the entire contents of the pan into the crock pot. 2. Add the tomatoes and white wine to the crock pot. Sprinkle with the oregano, basil, black pepper, paprika, and red pepper flakes. 3. Cover and cook on low for 4 to 5 hours, or on high for 2 to 3 hours. The mixture is done cooking when mushrooms are fork tender. 4. Clean and debeard the mussels. Discard any open

mussels. 5. Increase the heat on the crock pot to high once the mushroom mixture is done. Add the cleaned mussels to the crock pot and secure the lid tightly. Cook for 30 more minutes. 6. To serve, ladle the mussels into bowls with plenty of broth. Discard any mussels that didn't open up during cooking. Serve hot, with crusty bread for sopping up the sauce.

Mediterranean Cod au Gratin

Prep time: 20 minutes | Cook time: 1 hour | Serves 6

- 6 tablespoons olive oil
- 3 tablespoons all-purpose flour
- 1½ teaspoons sea salt
- ½ tablespoon dry mustard
- 1 teaspoon rosemary
- ¼ tablespoon ground nutmeg
- 1¼ cups milk
- 2 teaspoons lemon juice
- ⅓ cup grated Parmesan cheese
- ⅓ cup grated Asiago cheese
- ⅓ cup grated Romano cheese
- 3 pounds (1.4 kg) Pacific cod fillets

Make the Orange Layer: 1. Heat the olive oil in a small saucepan over medium heat. Stir in the flour, salt, mustard, rosemary, and nutmeg. 2. Gradually add the milk, stirring constantly until thickened. 3. Add the lemon juice, and the Parmesan, Asiago, and Romano cheeses to the saucepan. Stir until the cheeses are melted. 4. Place the fish into the crock pot, and spoon the cheese sauce over the fish. Cover and cook on high for 1 to 1½ hours or until the fish flakes. Serve hot.

Low Country Seafood Boil

Prep time: 15 minutes | Cook time: 6 hours | Serves 8

- 8 medium red potatoes
- 2 large, sweet onions, such as Vidalia, quartered
- 2 pounds (907 g) smoked sausage, cut into 3-inch pieces
- 1 (3-ounce / 85-g) package seafood boil seasoning
- 1 (12-ounce / 340-g) bottle pale ale beer
- 10 cups water
- 4 ears of corn, halved
- 2 pounds (907 g) medium raw shrimp, shelled and deveined
- Cocktail sauce, for serving
- Hot sauce, for serving
- ½ cup melted butter, for serving
- 1 large lemon, cut into wedges, for garnish

1. In the crock pot, put the potatoes, onions, smoked sausage, seafood boil seasoning, beer, and water. Stir to combine. Cover and cook for 6 hours, or until the potatoes are tender when pierced with a fork. 2. About 45 minutes before serving, add the corn. Cover and continue cooking for 25 minutes. Add the shrimp, cover, and continue cooking until the shrimp are pink and no longer translucent. 3. Drain the crock pot, discard the cooking liquid, and serve the seafood with cocktail sauce, hot sauce, melted butter, and lemon wedges.

Seafood Stew

Prep time: 15 minutes | Cook time: 6 hours | Serves 8

- 1 pound (454 g) waxy baby potatoes, such as Yukon Gold
- 2 medium onions, finely chopped
- 2 celery stalks, finely chopped
- 5 garlic cloves, minced
- 1 (28-ounce / 794-g) can crushed tomatoes
- 1 (8-ounce / 227-g) bottle clam juice
- 8 ounces (227 g) low-sodium fish stock
- 1 (6-ounce / 170-g) can tomato paste
- 1 tablespoon balsamic vinegar
- 1 teaspoon sugar
- ½ teaspoon celery salt
- ½ teaspoon kosher salt, plus more for seasoning
- ½ teaspoon freshly ground black pepper, plus more for seasoning
- 2 bay leaves
- 1 pound (454 g) firm-fleshed white fish, such as cod, cut into 1-inch pieces
- ½ pound (227 g) medium uncooked shrimp, shelled and deveined
- ½ pound (227 g) scallops, small side muscle removed, halved
- ¼ cup finely chopped flat-leaf parsley, for garnish

1. To the crock pot, add the potatoes, onions, celery, garlic, tomatoes, clam juice, fish stock, tomato paste, vinegar, sugar, celery salt, kosher salt, pepper, and bay leaves. Stir to combine. Cover and cook on low for 6 hours, or until the potatoes are tender when pierced with a fork. 2. About 30 minutes before serving, add the white fish, shrimp, and scallops. Cover and continue cooking on low until cooked through. 3. Discard the bay leaves. Season with additional salt and pepper, as needed. Ladle the stew into bowls, garnish with the parsley, and serve immediately.

South-of-the-Border Halibut

Prep time: 10 minutes | Cook time: 3½ hours | Serves 6

- 3 cups prepared medium-hot salsa
- 2 tablespoons fresh lime juice
- 1 teaspoon ground cumin
- 2 to 3 pounds (907 g to 1.4
- kg) halibut fillets
- 1½ cup finely shredded Monterey Jack cheese (or Pepper Jack for a spicy topping)

1. Combine the salsa, lime juice, and cumin in the insert of a 5- to 7-quart crock pot and stir. Cover the crock pot and cook on low for 2 hours. 2. Put the halibut in the cooker and spoon some of the sauce over the top of the fish. Sprinkle the cheese evenly over the fish. Cover and cook for an additional 30 to 45 minutes. 3. Remove the halibut from the crock pot and serve on a bed of the sauce.

Smoked Salmon and Potato Casserole

Prep time: 10 minutes | Cook time: 8 hours | Serves 2

- 1 teaspoon butter, at room temperature, or extra-virgin olive oil
- 2 eggs
- 1 cup 2% milk
- 1 teaspoon dried dill
- ⅛ teaspoon sea salt
- Freshly ground black pepper
- 2 medium russet potatoes, peeled and sliced thin
- 4 ounces (113 g) smoked salmon

1. Grease the inside of the crock pot with the butter. 2. In a small bowl, whisk together the eggs, milk, dill, salt, and a few grinds of the black pepper. 3. Spread one-third of the potatoes in a single layer on the bottom of the crock pot and top them with one-third of the salmon. Pour one-third of the egg mixture over the salmon. Repeat this layering with the remaining potatoes, salmon, and egg mixture. 4. Cover and cook on low for 8 hours or overnight.

Catalan-Style Seafood Stew

Prep time: 20 minutes | Cook time: 7 hours | Serves 6 to 8

- ½ cup extra-virgin olive oil
- 2 medium onions, finely chopped
- 2 medium red bell peppers, seeded and finely chopped
- 6 cloves garlic, minced
- 1 teaspoon saffron threads, crushed
- 1 teaspoon hot paprika
- 1 cup finely chopped Spanish chorizo or soppressata salami
- 1 (28- to 32-ounce / 794-
- to 907-g) can crushed tomatoes
- 2 cups clam juice
- 1 cup chicken broth
- 2 pounds (907 g) firm-fleshed fish, such as halibut, monkfish, cod, or sea bass fillets, cut into 1-inch chunks
- 1½ pounds (680 g) littleneck clams
- ½ cup finely chopped fresh Italian parsley

1. Heat the oil in a large skillet over medium-high heat. Add the onions, bell peppers, garlic, saffron, paprika, and chorizo and sauté until the vegetables are softened, 5 to 7 minutes. Add the tomatoes and transfer the contents of the skillet to the insert of a 5- to 7-quart crock pot. Add the clam juice and broth and stir to combine. 2. Cover and cook on low for 6 hours. Add the fish and clams to the crock pot insert, spooning some of the sauce over the fish and pushing the clams under the sauce. 3. Cover and cook for an additional 45 to 50 minutes, until the clams have opened and the fish is cooked through and opaque. Discard any clams that haven't opened. 4. Sprinkle the parsley over the stew and serve immediately.

Garlic Tilapia

Prep time: 5 minutes | Cook time: 2 hours | Serves 4

- 2 tablespoons butter, at room temperature
- 2 cloves garlic, minced
- 2 teaspoons minced fresh
- flat-leaf parsley
- 4 tilapia fillets
- Sea salt
- Black pepper

1. In a small bowl, mix the butter, garlic, and parsley to combine. 2. Pull out a large sheet of aluminum foil and put it on the counter. Place the fillets in the middle of the foil. 3. Season the fish generously with salt and pepper. 4. Evenly divide the butter mixture among the fillets and place on top. 5. Wrap the foil around the fish, sealing all sides and crimping the edges to make a packet. Place in the crock pot, cover, and cook on high for 2 hours. Serve hot.

Mahi-Mahi with Pineapple-Mango-Strawberry Salsa and Lentils

Prep time: 30 minutes | Cook time: 6 hours | Serves 6

- 1¼ cups vegetable or chicken stock
- 1 cup orange juice
- ¾ cup orange lentils
- ½ cup finely diced carrot
- ¼ cup finely diced red onion
- ¼ cup finely diced celery
- 1 tablespoon honey
- 6 (4- to-5-ounce / 113- to 142-g) mahi-mahi fillets
- Sea salt
- Black pepper
- 1 teaspoon lemon juice
- Salsa:
- ¾ cup finely diced pineapple
- ¾ cup finely diced mango
- ½ cup finely diced strawberries
- ¼ cup finely diced red onion
- 2 tablespoons chopped fresh mint (or 2 teaspoons dried)
- 2 tablespoons orange juice
- 1 tablespoon lime juice
- ¼ teaspoon salt

1. Combine the stock, orange juice, lentils, carrot, onion, celery, and honey in the crock pot. 2. Cover and cook on low for 5 to 5½ hours, or until the lentils are tender. 3. Place 1 sheet of parchment paper over the lentils in the crock pot. Season mahi-mahi lightly with salt and black pepper and place it on the parchment (skin-side down, if you have not removed the skin). Replace the lid and continue to cook on low for 25 minutes or until the mahi-mahi is opaque in the center. Remove the fish by lifting out the parchment paper and putting it on a plate. 4. Stir the lemon juice into the lentils and season with salt and pepper. Make the Salsa: 5. While the fish is cooking, combine the pineapple, mango, strawberries, red onion, mint, orange juice, lime juice, and salt into a big jar. Combine and chill to give the flavors a chance to blend. 6. To serve, place about ½ cup of hot lentils on a plate and top with a mahimahi fillet and ⅓ cup of salsa.

Honeyed Salmon

Prep time: 10 minutes | Cook time: 1 hour | Serves 6

- 6 (6-ounce / 170-g) salmon fillets
- ½ cup honey
- 2 tablespoons lime juice
- 3 tablespoons
- Worcestershire sauce
- 1 tablespoon water
- 2 cloves garlic, minced
- 1 teaspoon ground ginger
- ½ teaspoon black pepper

1. Place the salmon fillets in the crock pot. 2. In medium bowl, whisk the honey, lime juice, Worcestershire sauce, water, garlic, ginger, and pepper. Pour sauce over salmon. 3. Cover and cook on high for 1 hour.

Moroccan Sea Bass

Prep time: 20 minutes | Cook time: 3 to 4 hours | Serves 8

- 2 tablespoons extra-virgin olive oil
- 1 large yellow onion, finely chopped
- 1 medium red bell pepper, cut into ½-inch strips
- 1 medium yellow bell pepper, cut into ½-inch strips
- 4 garlic cloves, minced
- 1 teaspoon saffron threads, crushed in the palm of your hand
- 1½ teaspoons sweet paprika
- ¼ teaspoon hot paprika or ¼ teaspoon smoked paprika
- (or pimentón)
- ½ teaspoon ground ginger
- 1 (15-ounce / 425-g) can diced tomatoes, with the juice
- ¼ cup fresh orange juice
- 2 pounds (907 g) fresh sea bass fillets
- ¼ cup finely chopped fresh flat-leaf parsley
- ¼ cup finely chopped fresh cilantro
- Sea salt
- Black pepper
- 1 navel orange, thinly sliced, for garnish

1. In a large skillet, heat the olive oil over medium-high heat. Add the onion, red and yellow bell peppers, garlic, saffron, sweet paprika, hot or smoked paprika, and ginger and cook, stirring often, for 3 minutes, or until the onion begins to soften. 2. Add the tomatoes and stir for another 2 minutes, to blend the flavors. 3. Transfer the mixture to the crock pot and stir in the orange juice. 4. Place the sea bass fillets on top of the tomato mixture, and spoon some of the mixture over the fish. Cover and cook on high for 2 hours, or on low for 3 to 4 hours. At the end of the cooking time, the sea bass should be opaque in the center. 5. Carefully lift the fish out of the crock pot with a spatula and transfer to a serving platter. Cover loosely with aluminum foil. 6. Skim off any excess fat from the sauce, stir in the parsley and cilantro, and season with salt and pepper. 7. Spoon some of the sauce over the fish, and garnish with the orange slices. Serve hot, passing the remaining sauce on the side.

Garlic Crab Claws

Prep time: 10 minutes | Cook time: 5½ hours | Serves 6 to 8

- 1 cup (2 sticks) unsalted butter
- ½ cup olive oil
- 10 cloves garlic, sliced
- 2 tablespoons Old Bay seasoning
- 2 cups dry white wine or vermouth
- 1 lemon, thinly sliced
- 3 to 4 pounds (1.4 to 1.8 kg) cooked crab legs and claws, cracked

1. Put the butter, oil, garlic, seasoning, wine, and lemon in the insert of a 5- to 7-quart crock pot. 2. Cover and cook on low for 4 hours. Add the crab, spoon the sauce over the crab, and cook for an additional 1½ hours, turning the crab in the sauce during cooking. 3. Serve the crab from the cooker set on warm.

Poached Salmon Cakes in White Wine Butter Sauce

Prep time: 15 minutes | Cook time: 5 hours | Serves 6

- White Wine Butter Sauce:
- ½ cup (1 stick) unsalted butter
- 1 teaspoon Old Bay seasoning
- 2 cloves garlic, sliced
- 2 ½ cups white wine or vermouth
- Salmon Cakes:
- 4 cups cooked salmon, flaked
- 1 (6-ounce / 170-g) jar marinated artichoke hearts, drained and coarsely chopped
- 1 cup fresh bread crumbs
- ½ cup freshly grated Parmigiano-Reggiano cheese
- 1 large egg, beaten
- ½ teaspoon freshly ground black pepper

1. Put all the sauce ingredients in the insert of a 5- to 7-quart crock pot and stir to combine. Cover and cook on low for 4 hours. 2. Put all the salmon cake ingredients in a large mixing bowl and stir to combine. Form the mixture into 2-inch cakes. Place the cakes in the simmering sauce and spoon the sauce over the cakes. 3. Cover and cook for an additional 1 hour, until the cakes are tender. Carefully remove the cakes to a serving platter. 4. Strain the sauce through a fine-mesh sieve into a saucepan. Bring the sauce to a boil and reduce by half. 5. Serve the sauce over the cakes, or serve on the side.

Poached Salmon Provenç

Prep time: 15 minutes | Cook time: 1½ to 2 hours | Serves 6

- 3 pounds (1.4 kg) salmon fillets
- ½ cup dry white wine or vermouth
- 4 cloves garlic, peeled
- 1½ teaspoons finely chopped fresh rosemary
- 2 teaspoons finely chopped fresh thyme leaves
- 2 teaspoons finely chopped fresh tarragon
- ½ cup olive oil
- 1 (28- to 32-ounce / 794- to 907-g) can plum tomatoes, drained
- ½ cup heavy cream
- Salt and freshly ground black pepper

1. Place the salmon in the insert of a 5- to 7-quart crock pot and pour in the white wine. 2. Put the garlic, rosemary, thyme, tarragon, oil, and tomatoes in a food processor and process until smooth. Spoon the mixture over the salmon in the crock pot insert. 3. Cover and cook on high for 1½ to 2 hours, until the fish is cooked through. 4. Transfer the salmon from the crock pot insert to a serving platter and remove the skin. transfer the sauce to a saucepan and bring to a boil, reducing the sauce by about ¼ cup. Add the heavy cream and stir to combine. Season with the salt and pepper. 5. Serve the salmon and top with some of the sauce.

Shrimp with Marinara Sauce

Prep time: 15 minutes | Cook time: 6 to 7 hours | Serves 4

- 1 (15-ounce / 425-g) can diced tomatoes, with the juice
- 1 (6-ounce / 170-g) can tomato paste
- 1 clove garlic, minced
- 2 tablespoons minced fresh flat-leaf parsley
- ½ teaspoon dried basil
- 1 teaspoon dried oregano
- 1 teaspoon garlic powder
- 1½ teaspoons sea salt
- ¼ teaspoon black pepper
- 1 pound (454 g) cooked shrimp, peeled and deveined
- 2 cups hot cooked spaghetti or linguine, for serving
- ½ cup grated Parmesan cheese, for serving

1. Combine the tomatoes, tomato paste, and minced garlic in the crock pot. Sprinkle with the parsley, basil, oregano, garlic powder, salt, and pepper. 2. Cover and cook on low for 6 to 7 hours. 3. Turn up the heat to high, stir in the cooked shrimp, and cover and cook on high for about 15 minutes longer. 4. Serve hot over the cooked pasta. Top with Parmesan cheese.

Simple Poached Turbot

Prep time: 10 minutes | Cook time: 40 to 50 minutes | Serves 4

- 1 cup vegetable or chicken stock
- ½ cup dry white wine
- 1 yellow onion, sliced
- 1 lemon, sliced
- 4 sprigs fresh dill
- ½ teaspoon sea salt
- 4 (6-ounce / 170-g) turbot fillets

1. Combine the stock and wine in the crock pot. Cover and heat on high for 20 to 30 minutes. 2. Add the onion, lemon, dill, salt, and turbot to the crock pot. Cover and cook on high for about 20 minutes, until the turbot is opaque and cooked through according to taste. Serve hot.

Bouillabaisse

Prep time: 25 minutes | Cook time: 7 to 9 hours | Serves 6 to 8

- ¼ cup extra-virgin olive oil
- 3 leeks, cleaned and coarsely chopped, using the white and tender green parts
- 4 cloves garlic, sliced
- 1 bulb fennel, ends trimmed, coarsely chopped
- Grated zest of 1 orange
- 1 teaspoon dried thyme
- 1 teaspoon saffron threads, crushed
- Pinch of cayenne pepper
- 1 (28- to 32-ounce / 794- to 907-g) can crushed tomatoes, with their juice
- ½ cup white wine or dry vermouth
- 3 cups clam juice
- 1 cup chicken broth
- ½ pound (227 g) littleneck clams
- ½ pound (227 g) mussels
- 3 pounds (1.4 kg) thick-fleshed fish, cut into 1-inch chunks
- ½ cup finely chopped fresh Italian parsley

1. Heat the oil in a large skillet over medium-high heat. Add the leeks, garlic, fennel, zest, thyme, saffron, and cayenne and sauté until the vegetables are softened, about 2 minutes. Add the tomatoes and wine and cook down for 10 minutes, to concentrate the flavors. Transfer the mixture to the insert of a 5- to 7-quart crock pot. 2. Add the clam juice and broth to the crock pot insert and stir to combine. Cover and cook on low for 6 to 8 hours. Remove the cover and place the clams and mussels in the sauce. 3. Place the fish on top of the shellfish and spoon the sauce over the top of the fish. Cover and cook on high for 45 minutes, until the fish is cooked through and opaque and the clams and mussels have opened. 4. Discard any clams and mussels that haven't opened. Sprinkle with the parsley and serve immediately.

Beantown Scallops

Prep time: 10 minutes | Cook time: 4½ hours | Serves 6

- 1 cup (2 sticks) unsalted butter
- 2 tablespoons olive oil
- 2 cloves garlic, minced
- 2 teaspoons sweet paprika
- ¼ cup dry sherry
- 2 pounds (907 g) dry-pack sea scallops
- ½ cup finely chopped fresh Italian parsley

1. Put the butter, oil, garlic, paprika, and sherry in the insert of a 5- to 7-quart slower cooker. 2. Cover and cook on low for 4 hours. Turn the cooker to high and add the scallops, tossing them in the butter sauce. Cover and cook on high for 30 to 40 minutes, until the scallops are opaque. 3. Transfer the scallops and sauce from the crock pot to a serving platter. Sprinkle with the parsley and serve.

Seafood Laksa

Prep time: 30 minutes | Cook time: 2½ hours | Serves 6 to 8

- 2 tablespoons virgin coconut oil or extra-virgin olive oil
- 1 small onion, chopped
- 4 Thai bird chiles
- 1 (2-inch) piece fresh ginger, peeled and grated
- 1 (1-inch) piece fresh turmeric, peeled and grated
- 1 lemongrass stalk, tough outer leaves discarded, inner bulb chopped
- ¼ cup fresh cilantro
- 1 tablespoon tamarind paste
- ½ teaspoon ground cumin
- ½ teaspoon paprika
- 2 teaspoon coarse salt
- 2 cups unsweetened coconut milk
- 2 cups boiling water
- 4 kaffir lime leaves
- 2 teaspoon fish sauce
- 1 pound (454 g) medium shrimp, peeled and deveined (shells rinsed and reserved)
- 2 pounds (907 g) small mussels, scrubbed
- ¾ pound (340 g) firm fish fillet, such as halibut or cod, cut into 1-inch pieces
- 8 ounces (227 g) rice noodles
- Lime wedges, cubed firm tofu, sliced scallions, sliced Thai bird chiles, cilantro, and chili oil, for serving

1. Preheat a 7-quart crock pot. 2. Heat oil in a saucepan over medium. Add onion and cook until translucent, about 5 minutes. Add chiles, ginger, turmeric, lemongrass, cilantro, tamarind paste, cumin, paprika, and salt. Cook until fragrant, about 2 more minutes. Remove from heat and let cool. Transfer spice mixture to a food processor and puree to a thick paste. 3. Combine laksa paste, coconut milk, the boiling water, lime leaves, fish sauce, and shrimp shells in the crock pot. Cover and cook on low for 2 hours (we prefer this recipe on low). 4. Strain liquid through a medium sieve into a bowl, pressing down on solids; return broth to crock pot (discard solids). Add shrimp and mussels, and cook on low 20 minutes. Add fish and cook until shrimp is completely cooked through, fish is firm, and mussels open, about 10 minutes. 5. Meanwhile, prepare noodles according to package instructions. 6. To serve, divide noodles among bowls. Add broth and seafood, and top with tofu, scallions, chiles, and cilantro. Serve with lime wedges and chili oil.

Chapter 6

Stews and Soups

Creamy Tomato Soup

Prep time: 20 minutes | Cook time: 1½ hours | Serves 6

- 1 (26-ounce / 737-g) can condensed tomato soup, plus 6 ounces (170 g) water to equal 1 quart
- ½ teaspoon salt (optional)
- Half a stick butter
- 8 tablespoons flour
- 1 quart milk (whole or reduced-fat)

1. Put tomato soup, salt if you wish, and butter in crock pot. Blend well. 2. Cover and cook on high for 1 hour. 3. Meanwhile, place flour and 1 cup milk in 2-quart microwave-safe container. Whisk together until big lumps disappear. Then whisk in remaining milk until only small lumps remain. 4. Place flour-milk mixture in microwave and cook on high for 3 minutes. Remove and stir until smooth. Return to microwave and cook on high for another 3 minutes. 5. Add thickened milk slowly to hot soup in crock pot. 6. Heat thoroughly for 10 to 15 minutes.

Quick-to-Mix Vegetable Soup

Prep time: 5 minutes | Cook time: 5 to 7 hours | Serves 4

- 2 cups frozen vegetables
- ¾ cup fat-free, low-sodium beef gravy
- 1 (16-ounce / 454-g) can diced tomatoes
- ¼ cup dry red wine
- ½ cup diced onions
- 1 teaspoon crushed garlic
- ¼ teaspoon black pepper
- ½ cup water

1. Combine all ingredients in crock pot. 2. Cover. Cook on high 5 hours or on low 7 hours.

Curry Chicken Stew

Prep time: 15 minutes | Cook time: 4 hours | Serves 6

- 2 (14½-ounce / 411-g) cans chicken broth
- 1 (10¾-ounce / 305-g) can condensed cream of chicken soup, undiluted
- 1 tub Knorr concentrated chicken stock
- 4 garlic cloves, minced
- 1 tablespoon curry powder
- ¼ teaspoon salt
- ¼ teaspoon cayenne pepper
- ¼ teaspoon pepper
- 6 (6-ounce / 170-g) boneless skinless chicken breasts
- 1 medium green pepper, cut into thin strips
- 1 medium onion, thinly sliced
- Hot cooked rice
- Chopped fresh cilantro and chutney (optional)

1. In a large bowl, combine the first eight ingredients. Place chicken, green pepper and onion in a 5- or 6-quart crock pot; pour broth mixture over top. Cook, covered, on low 4 to 5 hours or until chicken and vegetables are tender. 2. Remove chicken and cool slightly. Cut or shred meat into bite-size pieces and return to crock pot; heat through. Serve with rice. If desired, top with cilantro and chutney.

The-Kasbah Chicken Vegetable Soup with Couscous

Prep time: 20 minutes | Cook time: 6 hours | Serves 8

- 2 tablespoons olive oil
- 1 medium onion, finely chopped
- 1 teaspoon ground cumin
- 1 teaspoon sweet paprika
- ¼ teaspoon ground cinnamon
- Pinch of cayenne pepper
- 2 medium zucchini, diced
- 2 medium yellow squash, diced
- 1 (14- to 15-ounce / 397- to 425-g) can diced tomatoes, with their juice
- 6 cups chicken broth
- 3 cups shredded cooked chicken
- ½ cup golden raisins
- 3 cups cooked couscous

1. Heat the oil in a large skillet over medium-high heat. 2. Add the onion, cumin, paprika, cinnamon, and cayenne and sauté until the onion begins to soften, about 3 minutes. Add the zucchini, squash, and tomatoes and toss to coat with the spices and onion. 3. Transfer the contents of the skillet to the insert of a 5- to 7-quart crock pot. Stir in the broth, chicken, and raisins. 4. Cover and cook on low for 6 hours, until the chicken and vegetables are tender. 5. Serve the soup over couscous in individual bowls.

Chicken-Nacho Soup

Prep time: 15 minutes | Cook time: 6 hours | Serves 8

- 3 tablespoons extra-virgin olive oil, divided
- 1 pound (454 g) ground chicken
- 1 sweet onion, diced
- 1 red bell pepper, chopped
- 2 teaspoons minced garlic
- 2 tablespoons taco seasoning
- 4 cups chicken broth
- 2 cups coconut milk
- 1 tomato, diced
- 1 jalapeño pepper, chopped
- 2 cups shredded Cheddar cheese
- ½ cup sour cream, for garnish
- 1 scallion, white and green parts, chopped, for garnish

1. Lightly grease the insert of the crock pot with 1 tablespoon of the olive oil. 2. In a large skillet over medium-high heat, heat the remaining 2 tablespoons of the olive oil. Add the chicken and sauté until it is cooked through, about 6 minutes. 3. Add the onion, red bell pepper, garlic, and taco seasoning, and sauté for an additional 3 minutes. 4. Transfer the chicken mixture to the insert, and stir in the broth, coconut milk, tomato, and jalapeño pepper. 5. Cover and cook on low for 6 hours. 6. Stir in the cheese. 7. Serve topped with the sour cream and scallion.

Potato Soup with Possibilities

Prep time: 20 minutes | Cook time: 5 to 6 hours | Serves 6

- 5 cups homemade chicken broth, or 2 (14-ounce / 397-g) cans chicken broth, plus ½ soup can water
- 1 large onion, chopped
- 3 celery stalks, chopped, including leaves, if you like
- 6 large white potatoes, peeled, chopped, cubed, or sliced
- Salt and pepper to taste

1. Place all ingredients in crock pot. 2. Cover and cook on high 5 hours, or on low 6 hours, or until vegetables are soft but not mushy.

Best Everyday Stew

Prep time: 20 minutes | Cook time: 10 hours | Serves 8

- 2¼ pounds (1 kg) flank steak, 1½-inch thick
- 8 red potatoes, small to medium in size
- 10 baby carrots
- 1 large clove garlic, diced
- 1 medium to large onion, chopped
- 1 cup baby peas
- 3 ribs celery, cut in 1-inch pieces
- 3 cups cabbage, in chunks
- 2 (8-ounce / 227-g) cans low-sodium tomato sauce
- 1 tablespoon Worcestershire sauce
- 2 bay leaves
- ¼ to ½ teaspoon dried thyme, according to your taste preference
- ¼ to ½ teaspoon dried basil, according to your taste preference
- ¼ to ½ teaspoon dried marjoram, according to your taste preference
- 1 tablespoon parsley
- 2 cups water or more, if desired
- 4 cubes beef or vegetable bouillon

1. Trim flank steak of fat. Cut in 1½-inch cubes. 2. Brown slowly in nonstick skillet. Quarter potatoes. 3. Combine all ingredients in large crock pot. 4. Cover. Cook on high 1 hour. Turn to low and cook 9 additional hours.

Ham 'n Cheese Soup

Prep time: 15 minutes | Cook time: 6¼ to 8¼ hours | Serves 7

- 2 cups potatoes, cubed (you decide whether to peel or not)
- 1½ cups water
- 1½ cups cooked ham, cubed
- 1 large onion, chopped
- 3 tablespoons butter or margarine
- 3 tablespoons flour
- ¼ teaspoon black pepper
- 3 cups fat-free milk
- 6 ounces (170 g) low-fat shredded cheese
- 1 cup frozen broccoli, thawed and chopped

1. Combine all ingredients except cheese and broccoli in crock pot. 2. Cook on low 6 to 8 hours. 3. Add cheese and broccoli. Stir well. Cook an additional 15 minutes, or until cheese is melted and broccoli is warm.

Tuscan Bean Soup with Herbs

Prep time: 15 minutes | Cook time: 8 hours | Serves 2

- 1 cup dried navy beans
- 1 onion, chopped
- 2 garlic cloves, minced
- 2 carrots, sliced
- 2 Yukon Gold potatoes, cubed
- 3 cups vegetable broth
- ½ teaspoon salt
- ⅛ teaspoon freshly ground black pepper
- ½ teaspoon dried thyme leaves
- 2 cups baby spinach leaves
- 2 teaspoons chopped fresh rosemary leaves
- 2 tablespoons chopped fresh flat-leaf parsley
- 2 tablespoons extra-virgin olive oil, divided

1. Sort the beans and rinse; drain well. 2. In the crock pot, combine the beans, onion, garlic, carrots, potatoes, broth, salt, pepper, and thyme. 3. Cover and cook on low for 7½ hours. 4. Add the spinach, rosemary, and parsley to the crock pot and stir. Cover and cook on low for 25 to 30 minutes more, or until the spinach wilts. 5. Ladle the soup into 2 bowls, drizzle each with 1 tablespoon of olive oil, and serve.

Turkey-Vegetable Stew

Prep time: 20 minutes | Cook time: 7 to 8 hours | Serves 6

- 3 tablespoons extra-virgin olive oil, divided
- 1 pound (454 g) boneless turkey breast, cut into 1-inch pieces
- 1 leek, thoroughly cleaned and sliced
- 2 teaspoons minced garlic
- 2 cups chicken broth
- 1 cup coconut milk
- 2 celery stalks, chopped
- 2 cups diced pumpkin
- 1 carrot, diced
- 2 teaspoons chopped thyme
- Salt, for seasoning
- Freshly ground black pepper, for seasoning
- 1 scallion, white and green parts, chopped, for garnish

1. Lightly grease the insert of the crock pot with 1 tablespoon of the olive oil. 2. In a large skillet over medium-high heat, heat the remaining 2 tablespoons of the olive oil. Add the turkey and sauté until browned, about 5 minutes. 3. Add the leek and garlic and sauté for an additional 3 minutes. 4. Transfer the turkey mixture to the insert and stir in the broth, coconut milk, celery, pumpkin, carrot, and thyme. 5. Cover and cook on low for 7 to 8 hours. 6. Season with salt and pepper. 7. Serve topped with the scallion.

Southwestern Bean Soup with Cornmeal Dumplings

Prep time: 20 minutes | Cook time: 4½ to 12½ hours | Serves 4

- Soup:
- 1 (15½-ounce / 439-g) can red kidney beans, rinsed and drained
- 1 (15½-ounce / 439-g) can black beans, pinto beans, or Great Northern beans, rinsed and drained
- 3 cups water
- 1 (14½-ounce / 411-g) can Mexican-style stewed tomatoes
- 1 (10-ounce / 283-g) package frozen whole-kernel corn, thawed
- 1 cup sliced carrots
- 1 cup chopped onions
- 1 (4-ounce / 113-g) can chopped green chilies
- 2 tablespoons instant beef, chicken, or vegetable bouillon granules
- 1 to 2 teaspoons chili powder
- 2 cloves garlic, minced
- Dumplings:
- ⅓ cup flour
- ¼ cup yellow cornmeal
- 1 teaspoon baking powder
- Dash of salt
- Dash of pepper
- 1 egg white, beaten
- 2 tablespoons milk
- 1 tablespoon oil

1. Combine 11 soup ingredients in crock pot. 2. Cover. Cook on low 10 to 12 hours, or on high 4 to 5 hours. 3. Make dumplings by mixing together flour, cornmeal, baking powder, salt, and pepper. 4. Combine egg white, milk, and oil. Add to flour mixture. Stir with fork until just combined. 5. At the end of the soup's cooking time, turn crock pot to high. Drop dumpling mixture by rounded teaspoonfuls to make 8 mounds atop the soup. 6. Cover. Cook for 30 minutes (do not lift cover).

Chicken Stock, the crock pot Method

Prep time: 20 minutes | Cook time: 4 to 10 hours | Makes about 6 cups

- 3 pounds (1.4 kg) chicken, skin removed
- 2 teaspoons salt
- 1 teaspoon freshly ground black pepper
- 3 tablespoons olive oil
- 2 large sweet onions, such as Vidalia, coarsely chopped
- ½ cup dry white wine
- 3 cups water
- 4 large carrots, peeled and cut into 2-inch chunks
- 4 stalks celery with some leaves, cut into 2-inch lengths
- 2 teaspoons dried thyme
- 1 teaspoon dried sage, crumbled

1. Sprinkle the chicken evenly with the salt and pepper. Heat the oil in a large skillet over high heat. Add the chicken and brown evenly on all sides. 2. Transfer the chicken to the insert of a 5- to 7-quart crock pot. Add the onions to the same skillet over medium-high heat and sauté until they begin to soften, about 3 minutes. 3. Transfer the onions to the crock pot insert. Deglaze the pan with the wine and bring the mixture to a boil. Add the water and scrape up any browned bits from the bottom of the pan. 4. Transfer the contents of the skillet to the crock pot insert. Add the carrots, celery, thyme, and sage to the insert. Cover and cook on high for 4 to 5 hours or on low for 8 to 10 hours. 5. Remove the chicken from the crock pot insert (it should be falling off the bone) with a slotted spoon and transfer to a plate or cutting board. Strain the stock through a fine-mesh sieve and discard any solids. Skim off any fat from the stock and store in refrigerator or freezer containers. 6. Remove the chicken meat from the bones, discarding the bones and any gristle or tendons. The meat can be used in soups, casseroles, or salads. Store the meat in the refrigerator for up to 2 days or in the freezer for up to 1 month.

Beef Barley Stew

Prep time: 15 minutes | Cook time: 9 to 10 hours | Serves 6

- ½ pound (227 g) lean round steak, cut in ½-inch cubes
- 4 carrots, peeled and cut in ¼-inch slices
- 1 cup chopped yellow onions
- ½ cup coarsely chopped green bell peppers
- 1 clove garlic, pressed
- ½ pound (227 g) fresh button mushrooms,
- quartered
- ¾ cup dry pearl barley
- ½ teaspoon salt
- ¼ teaspoon ground black pepper
- ½ teaspoon dried thyme
- ½ teaspoon dried sweet basil
- 1 bay leaf
- 5 cups fat-free, low-sodium beef broth

1. Combine all ingredients in crock pot. 2. Cover. Cook on low 9 to 10 hours.

Potato Soup with Spinach

Prep time: 20 minutes | Cook time: 8 hours | Serves 2

- 4 cups vegetable broth
- 2 russet potatoes, peeled and cubed
- 1 onion, chopped
- ½ cup chopped leeks
- 2 garlic cloves, minced
- ½ teaspoon salt
- ½ teaspoon dried marjoram
- ⅛ teaspoon freshly ground black pepper
- 2 cups baby spinach leaves

1. In the crock pot, combine the broth, potatoes, onion, leeks, garlic, salt, marjoram, and pepper, and stir. 2. Cover and cook on low for 7½ hours. 3. Using an immersion blender or potato masher, blend or mash the ingredients so the soup is fairly smooth but still has texture. 4. Add the spinach, cover, and cook on low for another 20 to 30 minutes, or until the spinach is wilted. 5. Ladle the soup into 2 bowls and serve.

Quick Clam and Corn Chowder

Prep time: 10 minutes | Cook time: 3 to 4 hours | Serves 4 to 6

- 2 (10½-ounce / 298-g) cans cream of potato soup
- 1 pint frozen corn
- 1 (6½-ounce / 184-g) can minced clams, drained
- 2 soup cans milk

1. Place all ingredients in crock pot. Stir to mix. 2. Cook on low 3 to 4 hours, or until hot.

Rutabaga and Sweet Potato Soup with Garlicky

Prep time: 10 minutes | Cook time: 8 hours | Serves 2

- 2 cups peeled, diced rutabaga
- 1 cup peeled, diced sweet potato
- 1 leek, white and pale green parts only, sliced thin
- ⅛ teaspoon sea salt
- 2 cups low-sodium vegetable broth
- 1 sprig fresh sage, plus 1 teaspoon minced fresh sage
- 1 teaspoon minced garlic
- 2 tablespoons toasted walnuts

1. Put the rutabaga, sweet potato, leek, salt, broth, and sprig of sage into the crock pot. 2. Cover and cook on low for 8 hours. Remove the sage sprig. 3. Use an immersion blender to purée the soup until smooth. 4. Place the 1 teaspoon minced fresh sage, garlic, and walnuts into a mortar and pestle and grind them into a paste. Serve each bowl of soup garnished with the walnut mixture.

Spiced-Pumpkin Chicken Soup

Prep time: 15 minutes | Cook time: 6 hours | Serves 6

- 1 tablespoon extra-virgin olive oil
- 4 cups chicken broth
- 2 cups coconut milk
- 1 pound (454 g) pumpkin, diced
- ½ sweet onion, chopped
- 1 tablespoon grated fresh ginger
- 2 teaspoons minced garlic
- ½ teaspoon ground

- cinnamon
- ¼ teaspoon ground nutmeg
- ¼ teaspoon freshly ground black pepper
- ¼ teaspoon salt
- Pinch ground allspice
- 1 cup heavy (whipping) cream
- 2 cups chopped cooked chicken

1. Lightly grease the insert of the crock pot with the olive oil. 2. Place the broth, coconut milk, pumpkin, onion, ginger, garlic, cinnamon, nutmeg, pepper, salt, and allspice in the insert. 3. Cover and cook on low for 6 hours. 4. Using an immersion blender or a regular blender, purée the soup. 5. If you removed the soup from the insert to purée, add it back to the pot, and stir in the cream and chicken. 6. Keep heating the soup on low for 15 minutes to heat the chicken through, and then serve warm.

Sauerkraut Potato Soup

Prep time: 15 minutes | Cook time: 2 to 8 hours | Serves 8

- 1 pound (454 g) smoked Polish sausage, cut into ½-inch pieces
- 5 medium potatoes, cubed
- 2 large onions, chopped
- 2 large carrots, cut into ¼-inch slices
- 1 (42-ounce / 1.2-kg) can chicken broth
- 1 (32-ounce / 907-g) can or bag sauerkraut, rinsed and drained
- 1 (6-ounce / 170-g) can tomato paste

1. Combine all ingredients in large crock pot. Stir to combine. 2. Cover. Cook on high 2 hours, and then on low 6 to 8 hours. 3. Serve.

Many-Veggies Beef Stew

Prep time: 25 minutes | Cook time: 10 to 11 hours | Serves 14 to 18

- 2 to 3 pounds (907 g to 1.4 kg) beef, cubed
- 1 (16-ounce / 454-g) package frozen green beans or mixed vegetables
- 1 (16-ounce / 454-g) package frozen corn
- 1 (16-ounce / 454-g) package frozen peas
- 2 pounds (907 g) carrots, chopped
- 1 large onion, chopped
- 4 medium potatoes, peeled and chopped
- 1 (10¾-ounce / 305-g) can tomato soup
- 1 (10¾-ounce / 305-g) can celery soup
- 1 (10¾-ounce / 305-g) can mushroom soup
- Bell pepper, chopped (optional)

1. Combine all ingredients in 2 (4-quart) crock pots (this is a very large recipe). 2. Cover. Cook on low 10 to 11 hours.

Vegetable Soup with Noodles

Prep time: 15 minutes | Cook time: 2 to 6 hours | Serves 6

- 1 pint water
- 2 beef bouillon cubes
- 1 onion, chopped
- 1 pound (454 g) ground beef
- ¼ cup ketchup
- 1 teaspoon salt
- ⅛ teaspoon celery salt
- ½ cup noodles, uncooked
- 1 (16-ounce / 454-g) package frozen mixed vegetables, or vegetables of your choice
- 1 pint tomato juice

1. Dissolve bouillon cubes in water. 2. Brown onion and beef in skillet. Drain. 3. Combine all ingredients in crock pot. 4. Cover. Cook on low 6 hours, or on high 2 to 3 hours, until vegetables are tender.

Saigon Chicken Rice Soup

Prep time: 15 minutes | Cook time: 6 hours | Serves 8

- 8 cups chicken broth
- 4 chicken breast halves, skin and bones removed
- 3 dime-size thin slices fresh ginger
- 1 tablespoon soy sauce
- 1 teaspoon Asian fish sauce
- 1 teaspoon chili garlic
- sauce
- ½ cup grated carrot
- 1 cup thinly sliced Napa cabbage
- 6 green onions, thinly sliced on a diagonal
- 2 cups cooked jasmine rice

1. Pour the broth into the insert of a 5- to 7-quart crock pot. 2. Place the chicken in the bottom of the crock pot insert with the broth and add the ginger, soy sauce, fish sauce, and chili sauce. Cover the cooker and cook on high for 4 hours. 3. Strain the broth through a fine-mesh sieve into a bowl, at the end of the 4 hours, and shred the chicken. 4. Return the chicken and broth to the crock pot insert and add the carrot, cabbage, green onions, and rice. Keep warm on low for up to 2 hours before serving. If the soup thickens, add more broth.

Steak and Mushroom Soup

Prep time: 20 minutes | Cook time: 6 to 7 hours | Serves 6 to 8

- 4 tablespoons (½ stick) unsalted butter
- 1 cup finely chopped shallots (about 6 medium)
- 1½ pounds (680 g) assorted mushrooms, tougher stems removed, cut into ½-inch-thick slices
- 2½ teaspoons salt
- 1 teaspoon freshly ground black pepper
- 1½ teaspoons dried thyme
- leaves
- 2½ to 3 pounds (1.1 to 1.4 kg) beef top sirloin, cut into ½-inch pieces
- ¼ cup cream sherry
- 4 cups beef broth
- 2 tablespoons cornstarch mixed with ¼ cup water or broth
- 1 cup heavy cream
- ½ cup finely chopped fresh Italian parsley

1. Melt 2 tablespoons of the butter in a large skillet over medium-high heat. Add the shallots and mushrooms and sprinkle them with ½ teaspoon of the salt, ½ teaspoon of the pepper, and the thyme. Sauté until the mushrooms start to color, 10 to 15 minutes. 2. Transfer the mushrooms to the insert of a 5- to 7-quart crock pot. Sprinkle the meat with the remaining 2 teaspoons salt and ½ teaspoon pepper. 3. Melt the remaining 2 tablespoons butter in the skillet over high heat. Add the meat a few pieces at a time and brown on all sides. 4. Transfer the browned meat to the crock pot insert. Deglaze the pan with the sherry and scrape up any browned bits from the bottom of the skillet. 5. Transfer the sherry to the insert and stir in the broth. Cover and cook the soup on low for 5 to 6 hours, until the meat is tender. 6. Add the cornstarch mixture and the cream to the soup and stir to combine. Cook for an additional 30 minutes, until the soup is thickened. 7. Stir in the parsley before serving.

Mixed Shellfish Chowder

Prep time: 20 minutes | Cook time: 5 hours | Serves 8

- 4 tablespoons (½ stick) unsalted butter
- 1 medium onion, finely chopped
- 3 stalks celery, finely chopped
- 1 teaspoon sweet paprika
- ½ teaspoon dried thyme
- 3 tablespoons all-purpose flour
- 6 cups lobster stock
- 2 tablespoons brandy
- ½ pound (227 g) cooked lobster meat, picked over for shells and cartilage
- ½ pound (227 g) lump crab meat, picked over for shells and cartilage
- ¼ pound (113 g) bay or sea scallops, cut into quarters
- 1 cup heavy cream
- ¼ cup finely chopped fresh chives, for garnish

1. Melt the butter in a saucepan over medium-high heat. Add the onion, celery, paprika, and thyme and sauté until the vegetables begin to soften, about 3 minutes. Stir in the flour and cook for 2 to 3 minutes, whisking the roux constantly. Stir in the stock and brandy and bring to a boil. 2. Transfer the contents of the skillet to the insert of a 5- to 7-quart crock pot. Cover and cook for 4 hours on low. Add the lobster, crab, scallops, and cream and cook on low for an additional 1 hour. 3. Serve the soup garnished with chives.

Chicken and Shrimp Bouillabaisse

Prep time: 20 minutes | Cook time: 7¼ hours | Serves 2

- 4 boneless, skinless chicken thighs, cut into strips
- 1 onion, chopped
- 3 garlic cloves, minced
- 1 cup sliced fennel
- 2 large tomatoes, seeded and chopped
- 2 Yukon Gold potatoes, cubed
- 2 cups clam juice
- ½ cup dry white wine
- 1 teaspoon dried thyme leaves
- ½ teaspoon salt
- ⅛ teaspoon freshly ground black pepper
- 1 pinch saffron
- ½ pound (227 g) medium shrimp, peeled and deveined
- 1 teaspoon minced fresh rosemary leaves

1. In the crock pot, combine all the ingredients except the shrimp and rosemary, and mix well. 2. Cover and cook on low for 7 hours. 3. Add the shrimp and rosemary. Cover and cook on high for 20 minutes, or until the shrimp curl and turn pink. 4. Ladle the stew into 2 bowls and serve.

Double Corn and Cheddar Chowder

Prep time: 10 minutes | Cook time: 4½ hours | Serves 6

- 1 tablespoon butter or margarine
- 1 cup onions, chopped
- 2 tablespoons all-purpose flour
- 2½ cups fat-free, reduced-sodium chicken broth
- 1 (16-ounce / 454-g) can creamed corn
- 1 cup frozen corn
- ½ cup finely chopped red bell peppers
- ½ teaspoon hot pepper sauce
- ¾ cup shredded, reduced-fat, sharp Cheddar cheese

1. In saucepan on top of stove, melt butter or margarine. Stir in onions and sauté until wilted. Stir in flour. When well mixed, whisk in chicken broth. Stir frequently over medium heat until broth is thickened. 2. Pour into crock pot. Mix in remaining ingredients except cheese. 3. Cook on low 4½ hours. About an hour before the end of the cooking time, stir in cheese until melted and well blended.

Shrimp Chowder

Prep time: 20 minutes | Cook time: 3½ to 4 hours | Serves 8

- 8 strips thick-cut bacon, cut into ½-inch pieces
- 1 large onion, finely chopped
- 4 stalks celery, finely chopped
- 1 teaspoon dried thyme
- 2 teaspoons Old Bay seasoning
- 3 tablespoons all-purpose flour
- 3 cups chicken broth
- 2 (8-ounce / 227-g) bottles clam juice
- 5 medium red or Yukon gold potatoes, cut into ½-inch chunks
- 1 bay leaf
- 1½ pounds (680 g) medium shrimp, peeled and deveined
- 1½ cups heavy cream
- ¼ cup finely chopped fresh Italian parsley, for garnish
- ¼ cup finely chopped fresh chives, for garnish

1. Cook the bacon in a large skillet over medium-high heat until crisp and remove it to paper towels to drain. Remove all but ¼ cup of the bacon drippings from the skillet. 2. Add the onion, celery, thyme, and seasoning and sauté until the onion is translucent, 5 to 7 minutes. Stir in the flour and cook for 3 minutes, whisking the roux constantly. Gradually stir in the broth and clam juice and bring to a boil. 3. Transfer the contents of the skillet to the insert of a 5- to 7-quart crock pot. Stir in the potatoes and bay leaf. Cover and cook on high for 2½ to 3 hours, until the potatoes are tender. Stir in the bacon, shrimp, and cream. 4. Cover and cook for an additional 45 minutes to 1 hour, until the shrimp is cooked through. 5. Remove the bay leaf and serve garnished with parsley and chives.

Chicken Corn Soup

Prep time: 15 minutes | Cook time: 8 to 9 hours | Serves 4 to 6

- 2 whole boneless, skinless chicken breasts, cubed
- 1 onion, chopped
- 1 garlic clove, minced
- 2 carrots, sliced
- 2 ribs celery, chopped
- 2 medium potatoes, cubed
- 1 teaspoon mixed dried herbs
- ⅓ cup tomato sauce
- 1 (12-ounce / 340-g) can cream-style corn
- 1 (14-ounce / 397-g) whole-kernel corn
- 3 cups chicken stock
- ¼ cup chopped Italian parsley
- 1 teaspoon salt
- ¼ teaspoon pepper

1. Combine all ingredients except parsley, salt, and pepper in crock pot. 2. Cover. Cook on low 8 to 9 hours, or until chicken is tender. 3. Add parsley and seasonings 30 minutes before serving.

Polish Sausage Stew

Prep time: 15 minutes | Cook time: 4 to 8 hours | Serves 6 to 8

- 1 (10¾-ounce / 305-g) can cream of celery soup
- ⅓ cup packed brown sugar
- 1 (27-ounce / 765-g) can sauerkraut, drained
- 1½ pounds (680 g) Polish sausage, cut into 2-inch pieces and browned
- 4 medium potatoes, cubed
- 1 cup chopped onions
- 1 cup shredded Monterey Jack cheese

1. Combine soup, sugar, and sauerkraut. Stir in sausage, potatoes, and onions. 2. Cover. Cook on low 8 hours, or on high 4 hours. 3. Stir in cheese and serve.

Mushroom Soup

Prep time: 10 minutes | Cook time: 8 hours | Serves 2

- 1 ounce (28 g) dried wild mushrooms
- 8 ounces (227 g) cremini mushrooms, washed and quartered
- 2 cups low-sodium chicken broth
- 2 tablespoons dry sherry (optional)
- 1 onion, halved, cut into thin half circles
- 2 garlic cloves, minced
- 1 teaspoon fresh thyme
- ½ teaspoon minced fresh rosemary
- ⅛ teaspoon sea salt
- ¼ cup heavy cream

1. Put the wild mushrooms, cremini mushrooms, broth, sherry (if using), onion, garlic, thyme, rosemary, and salt in the crock pot and stir to combine. 2. Cover and cook on low for 8 hours. 3. Stir in the heavy cream just before serving.

Creamy Corn Chowder

Prep time: 30 minutes | Cook time: 2 hours | Serves 12

- ½ pound (227 g) lean turkey bacon
- 4 cups diced potatoes
- 2 cups chopped onions
- 2 cups fat-free sour cream
- 1½ cups fat-free milk
- 2 (10¾-ounce / 305-g) cans
- fat-free, low-sodium cream of chicken soup
- 2 (15¼-ounce / 432-g) cans fat-free, low-sodium whole-kernel corn, undrained

1. Cut bacon into 1-inch pieces. Cook for 5 minutes in large nonstick skillet, doing it in two batches so all the pieces brown. 2. Add potatoes and onions and a bit of water. Cook 15 to 20 minutes, until vegetables are tender, stirring occasionally. Drain. Transfer to crock pot. 3. Combine sour cream, milk, chicken soup, and corn. Place in crock pot. 4. Cover. Cook on low for 2 hours.

Red Curry Butternut Squash Soup

Prep time: 15 minutes | Cook time: 8 hours | Serves 2

- 2 cups cubed butternut squash
- ½ cup diced onion
- 1 teaspoon minced garlic
- 1 teaspoon minced ginger
- 2 cups low-sodium chicken broth
- 1 teaspoon Thai red curry
- paste
- 1 teaspoon fish sauce
- ½ cup coconut milk
- 1 teaspoon freshly squeezed lime juice
- ¼ cup fresh cilantro, for garnish

1. Put the butternut squash, onion, garlic, ginger, broth, curry paste, fish sauce, and coconut milk in the crock pot. Stir gently to combine. 2. Cover and cook on low for 8 hours. 3. Just before serving, stir in the lime juice and garnish the soup with the cilantro.

Butternut Squash Soup

Prep time: 5 minutes | Cook time: 4 to 8 hours | Serves 4 to 6

- 1 (45-ounce / 1.3-kg) can chicken broth
- 1 medium butternut squash, peeled and cubed
- 1 small onion, chopped
- 1 teaspoon ground ginger
- 1 teaspoon garlic, minced (optional)
- ¼ teaspoon nutmeg (optional)

1. Place chicken broth and squash in crock pot. Add remaining ingredients. 2. Cover and cook on high 4 hours, or on low 6 to 8 hours, or until squash is tender.

Tasty Clam Chowder

Prep time: 15 minutes | Cook time: 2½ hours | Serves 8

- 2 (1-pound / 454-g) cans low-fat, low-sodium chicken broth
- 3 large potatoes, peeled and diced finely
- 2 large onions, chopped finely
- 1 (1-pound / 454-g) can creamed corn
- 1 carrot, chopped finely
- 1 dozen littleneck clams,
- or 3 (6-ounce / 170-g) cans minced clams
- 2 cups low-fat milk
- ¼ teaspoon black pepper
- ¼ teaspoon salt
- 2 tablespoons chopped fresh parsley
- 6 slices bacon, well cooked, drained and crumbled (optional)

1. Pour broth into crock pot. 2. Add potatoes, onions, creamed corn, and carrot. 3. Cover. Cook on high 1 hour. Stir. Cook on high another hour. 4. Using a potato masher, mash potatoes coarsely to thicken soup. 5. Add clams, milk, salt, black pepper, salt, and parsley. 6. Cover. Cook on high 20 minutes. 7. Garnish with crumbled bacon, if desired.

Sweet Spiced Lentil Soup

Prep time: 10 minutes | Cook time: 8 hours | Serves 2

- 1 cup dried lentils, rinsed and sorted
- 1 apple, cored, peeled, and diced
- 1 cup diced onion
- ¼ cup diced celery
- 1 teaspoon fresh thyme
- ¼ teaspoon ground cinnamon
- ¼ teaspoon ground allspice
- ⅛ teaspoon sea salt
- ¼ cup dry red wine
- 3 cups low-sodium chicken or vegetable broth

1. Put all the ingredients into the crock pot and stir to combine. 2. Cover and cook on low for 6 to 8 hours, until the lentils are very soft.

Black Bean and Corn Soup

Prep time: 10 minutes | Cook time: 5 to 6 hours | Serves 6 to 8

- 2 (15-ounce / 425-g) cans black beans, drained and rinsed
- 1 (14½-ounce / 411-g) can Mexican stewed tomatoes, undrained
- 1 (14½-ounce / 411-g) can diced tomatoes, undrained
- 1 (11-ounce / 312-g) can whole-kernel corn, drained
- 4 green onions, sliced
- 2 to 3 tablespoons chili powder
- 1 teaspoon ground cumin
- ½ teaspoon dried minced garlic

1. Combine all ingredients in crock pot. 2. Cover. Cook on high 5 to 6 hours.

Corn and Shrimp Chowder

Prep time: 20 minutes | Cook time: 3 to 4 hours | Serves 6

- 3 slices lean turkey bacon, diced
- 1 cup chopped onions
- 2 cups diced, unpeeled red potatoes
- 2 (10-ounce / 283-g) packages frozen corn
- 1 teaspoon Worcestershire sauce
- ½ teaspoon paprika
- ½ teaspoon salt
- ⅛ teaspoon black pepper
- 2 (6-ounce / 170-g) cans shrimp, drained
- 2 cups water
- 2 tablespoons butter
- 1 (12-ounce / 340-g) can fat-free evaporated milk
- Chopped chives

1. Brown bacon in nonstick skillet until lightly crisp. Add onions to drippings and sauté until transparent. Using slotted spoon, transfer bacon and onions to crock pot. 2. Add remaining ingredients to cooker except milk and chives. 3. Cover. Cook on low 3 to 4 hours, adding milk and chives 30 minutes before end of cooking time.

Reggiano

Prep time: 25 minutes | Cook time: 3 to 8 hours | Serves 8

- 2 tablespoons extra-virgin olive oil
- 3 cloves garlic, minced
- 1 cup coarsely chopped sweet onion
- 1 cup coarsely chopped carrots
- 1 cup coarsely chopped celery
- 1 tablespoon finely chopped fresh rosemary
- 1 (14- to 15-ounce / 397- to 425-g) can plum tomatoes, with their juice
- ¼ cup dry white wine
- 2 medium zucchini, cut into ½-inch rounds
- 1 (14- to 15-ounce / 397- to 425-g) can small white beans, drained and rinsed
- 1 head escarole or Savoy
- cabbage, cut into small pieces
- 8 ounces (227 g) green beans, ends snipped, cut into 1-inch pieces
- 1 medium head cauliflower, cut into florets
- Rind from Parmigiano-Reggiano cheese, cut into ½-inch pieces, plus ½ to 1 cup finely grated Parmigiano-Reggiano cheese, for garnish
- 2 cups vegetable broth
- 1 teaspoon salt
- ½ teaspoon freshly ground black pepper
- 8 ounces (227 g) cooked small pasta (shells, ditalini, or other short tubular pasta)

1. Heat the oil in a large skillet over medium-high heat. Add the garlic, onion, carrots, celery, and rosemary and sauté until the vegetables begin to soften, 4 to 5 minutes. 2. Add the tomatoes and wine and allow some of the liquid to evaporate in the pan.

3. Transfer the contents of the skillet to the insert of a 5- to 7-quart crock pot. Add the zucchini, white beans, cabbage, green beans, cauliflower, Parmigiano-Reggiano rind, broth, salt, and pepper. 4. Cover the crock pot and cook on high for 3 to 4 hours or on low for 6 to 8 hours. 5. Stir in the cooked pasta at the end of the cooking time, cover, and set on warm until ready to serve. 6. Serve the soup garnished with the grated Parmigiano-Reggiano.

Chicken Noodle Soup with Vegetables

Prep time: 15 minutes | Cook time: 5 to 7 hours | Serves 6

- 2 onions, chopped
- 2 cups sliced carrots
- 2 cups sliced celery
- 1 (10-ounce / 283-g) package frozen peas (optional)
- 2 teaspoons salt (optional)
- ¼ teaspoon black pepper
- ½ teaspoon dried basil
- ¼ teaspoon dried thyme
- 3 tablespoons dry parsley flakes
- 4 cups water
- 2½ to 3 pounds (1.1 to 1.4 kg) chicken, cut-up
- 1 cup thin noodles, uncooked

1. Place all ingredients in crock pot, except chicken and noodles. 2. Remove skin and any fat from chicken pieces. Then place chicken in cooker, on top of the rest of the ingredients. 3. Cover. Cook on high 4 to 6 hours. 4. One hour before serving, remove chicken. 5. Cool slightly. Cut meat from bones. Return meat to cooker. Add noodles. 6. Cover. Cook on high 1 hour.

Fennel and Tomato Soup

Prep time: 10 minutes | Cook time: 2 to 4 hours | Serves 6

- 2 tablespoons rapeseed oil
- 2 teaspoons fennel seeds
- 5 garlic cloves, sliced
- 2 fresh green chiles
- 1 teaspoon salt
- 1 pound (454 g) ripe tomatoes, roughly chopped
- Handful fresh coriander stems, roughly chopped
- 3 cups hot water
- 1 teaspoon fennel seeds, roasted and roughly crushed, for garnish

1. Preheat the crock pot on high. 2. Heat the oil in a frying pan (or in the crock pot if you have a sear setting) and add the fennel seeds. When they are sizzling, add the garlic and cook until it is just brown. Pour everything into the crock pot. 3. Throw in the whole green chiles and the salt. 4. Add the chopped tomatoes, coriander stems, and water. 5. Cook on low for 4 hours, or on high for 2 hours. 6. Using an immersion or regular blender, purée until smooth. 7. Pour into serving bowls and serve topped with a few toasted fennel seeds.

Lentil-Vegetable Soup

Prep time: 15 minutes | Cook time: 8 hours | Serves 2

- ½ cup dried lentils
- 1 cup chopped grape tomatoes
- 2 carrots, chopped
- 2 celery stalks, chopped
- 1 onion, chopped
- 3 garlic cloves, sliced
- 1 bay leaf
- ½ teaspoon dried thyme leaves
- ½ teaspoon dried marjoram
- ½ teaspoon salt
- 2 cups vegetable broth
- 1 cup water
- 2 tablespoons minced fresh thyme leaves

1. Sort the lentils and rinse; drain well. 2. In the crock pot, combine the lentils with all the remaining ingredients except the fresh thyme leaves. 3. Cover and cook on low for 8 hours, or until the lentils and vegetables are tender. 4. Remove and discard the bay leaf, stir in the fresh thyme leaves, ladle the soup into 2 bowls and serve.

Tasty Chicken Soup

Prep time: 15 minutes | Cook time: 6 to 7 hours | Serves 12

- 12 cups chicken broth
- 2 cups cooked chicken, cubed
- 1 cup shredded carrots
- 3 whole cloves
- Small onion
- 1 (16-ounce / 454-g) bag of dry noodles, cooked (optional)

1. Place broth, chicken, and carrots in crock pot. 2. Peel onion. Using a toothpick, poke 3 holes on the cut ends. Carefully press cloves into 3 of the holes until only their round part shows. Add to crock pot. 3. Cover and cook on high 6 to 7 hours. 4. If you'd like a thicker soup, add a bag of cooked fine egg noodles before serving.

Minestrone with Parmigiano-Russian Red-Lentil Soup

Prep time: 15 minutes | Cook time: 3¾ to 4¾ hours | Serves 8

- 1 tablespoon oil
- 1 large onion, chopped
- 3 cloves garlic, minced
- ½ cup diced, dried apricots
- 1½ cups dried red lentils
- ½ teaspoon cumin
- ½ teaspoon dried thyme
- 3 cups water
- 2 (14½-ounce / 411-g) cans chicken or vegetable broth
- 1 (14½-ounce / 411-g) can diced tomatoes
- 1 tablespoon honey
- ¾ teaspoon salt
- ½ teaspoon coarsely ground black pepper
- 2 tablespoons chopped fresh mint
- 1½ cups plain yogurt

1. Combine all ingredients except mint and yogurt in crock pot.

2. Cover. Heat on high until soup starts to simmer, then turn to low and cook 3 to 4 hours. 3. Add mint and dollop of yogurt to each bowl of soup.

Nancy's Vegetable Beef Soup

Prep time: 10 minutes | Cook time: 8 hours | Serves 6 to 8

- 1 (2-pound / 907-g) roast cut into bite-sized pieces, or 2 pounds (907 g) stewing meat
- 1 (15-ounce / 425-g) can corn
- 1 (15-ounce / 425-g) can green beans
- 1 (1-pound / 454-g) bag frozen peas
- 1 (40-ounce / 1.1-kg) can stewed tomatoes
- 5 beef bouillon cubes
- Tabasco to taste
- 2 teaspoons salt

1. Combine all ingredients in crock pot. Do not drain vegetables. 2. Add water to fill crock pot to within 3 inches of top 3. Cover. Cook on low 8 hours, or until meat is tender and vegetables are soft.

Green Bean and Ham Soup

Prep time: 15 minutes | Cook time: 4¼ to 6¼ hours | Serves 6

- 1 meaty ham bone, or 2 cups cubed ham
- 1½ quarts water
- 1 large onion, chopped
- 2 to 3 cups cut-up green beans
- 3 large carrots, sliced
- 2 large potatoes, peeled and cubed
- 1 tablespoon parsley
- 1 tablespoon summer savory
- ½ teaspoon salt
- ¼ teaspoon pepper
- 1 cup cream or milk

1. Combine all ingredients except cream in crock pot. 2. Cover. Cook on high 4 to 6 hours. 3. Remove ham bone. Cut off meat and return to crock pot. 4. Turn to low. Stir in cream or milk. Heat through and serve.

Split Pea Soup with Ham

Prep time: 15 minutes | Cook time: 4 hours | Serves 8

- 2½ quarts water
- 1 ham hock or pieces of cut-up ham
- 2½ cups split peas, dried
- 1 medium onion, chopped
- 3 medium carrots, cut in small pieces
- Salt and pepper to taste

1. Bring water to a boil in a saucepan on your stovetop. 2. Place all other ingredients into crock pot. Add water and stir together well. 3. Cover and cook on high for 4 hours, or until vegetables are tender. 4. If you've cooked a ham hock, remove it from the soup and debone the meat. Stir cut-up chunks of meat back into the soup before serving.

Green Bean and Sausage Soup

Prep time: 25 minutes | Cook time: 7 to 10 hours | Serves 5 to 6

- 1 medium onion, chopped
- 2 carrots, sliced
- 2 ribs celery, sliced
- 1 tablespoon olive oil
- 5 medium potatoes, cubed
- 1 (10-ounce / 283-g) package frozen green beans
- 2 (14½-ounce / 411-g) cans chicken broth
- 2 broth cans water
- ⅓ pound (151 g) link
- sausage, sliced, or bulk sausage, browned
- 2 tablespoons chopped fresh parsley, or 2 teaspoons dried
- 1 to 2 tablespoons chopped fresh oregano, or 1 to 2 teaspoons dried
- 1 teaspoon Italian spice
- Salt to taste
- Pepper to taste

1. Sauté onion, carrots, and celery in oil in skillet until tender. 2. Combine all ingredients in crock pot. 3. Cover. Cook on high 1 to 2 hours and then on low 6 to 8 hours. 4. Serve.

Curried Vegetable Stew

Prep time: 15 minutes | Cook time: 7 to 8 hours | Serves 6

- 1 tablespoon extra-virgin olive oil
- 4 cups coconut milk
- 1 cup diced pumpkin
- 1 cup cauliflower florets
- 1 red bell pepper, diced
- 1 zucchini, diced
- 1 sweet onion, chopped
- 2 teaspoons grated fresh ginger
- 2 teaspoons minced garlic
- 1 tablespoon curry powder
- 2 cups shredded spinach
- 1 avocado, diced, for garnish

1. Lightly grease the insert of the crock pot with the olive oil. 2. Add the coconut milk, pumpkin, cauliflower, bell pepper, zucchini, onion, ginger, garlic, and curry powder. 3. Cover and cook on low for 7 to 8 hours. 4. Stir in the spinach. 5. Garnish each bowl with a spoonful of avocado and serve.

Wild Rice Soup

Prep time: 15 minutes | Cook time: 4 to 6 hours | Serves 8

- 2 tablespoons butter
- ½ cup dry wild rice
- 6 cups fat-free, low-sodium chicken stock
- ½ cup minced onions
- ½ cup minced celery
- ½ pound (227 g) winter
- squash, peeled, seeded, cut in ½-inch cubes
- 2 cups cooked chicken, chopped
- ½ cup browned, slivered almonds

1. Melt butter in small skillet. Add rice and sauté for 10 minutes over low heat. Transfer to crock pot. 2. Add all remaining ingredients except chicken and almonds. 3. Cover. Cook on

low 4 to 6 hours. One hour before serving stir in chicken. 4. Top with browned slivered almonds just before serving.

Green Chili Stew

Prep time: 20 minutes | Cook time: 4 to 6 hours | Serves 6 to 8

- 3 tablespoons oil
- 2 garlic cloves, minced
- 1 large onion, diced
- 1 pound (454 g) ground sirloin
- ½ pound (227 g) ground pork
- 3 cups chicken broth
- 2 cups water
- 2 (4-ounce / 113-g) cans
- diced green chilies
- 4 large potatoes, diced
- 1 (10-ounce / 283-g) package frozen corn
- 1 teaspoon black pepper
- 1 teaspoon crushed dried oregano
- ½ teaspoon ground cumin
- 1 teaspoon salt

1. Brown onion, garlic, sirloin, and pork in oil in skillet. Cook until meat is no longer pink. 2. Combine all ingredients in crock pot. 3. Cover. Cook on low 4 to 6 hours, or until potatoes are soft.

Tempting Beef Stew

Prep time: 10 minutes | Cook time: 10 to 12 hours | Serves 10 to 12

- 2 to 3 pounds (907 g to 1.4 kg) beef stewing meat
- 3 carrots, thinly sliced
- 1 (1-pound / 454-g) package frozen green peas with onions
- 1 (1-pound / 454-g) package frozen green beans
- 1 (16-ounce / 454-g) can
- whole or stewed tomatoes
- ½ cup beef broth
- ½ cup white wine
- ½ cup brown sugar
- 4 tablespoons tapioca
- ½ cup bread crumbs
- 2 teaspoons salt
- 1 bay leaf
- Pepper to taste

1. Combine all ingredients in crock pot. 2. Cover. Cook on low 10 to 12 hours. 3. Serve.

Chapter 7
Vegetables and Sides

Apples and Sauerkraut

Prep time: 15 minutes | Cook time: 4 to 5 hours | Serves 6 to 8

- ½ cup (1 stick) unsalted butter
- 2 large onions, coarsely chopped
- ¼ cup sugar
- 6 cups finely shredded green cabbage (about 1 ½
- medium heads)
- 3 (15-ounce / 425-g) cans sauerkraut, rinsed, drained, and squeezed dry
- 2 medium Granny Smith apples, peeled, cored, and thinly sliced

1. Melt the butter in a large skillet over medium-high heat. Add the onions and sugar and sauté until the onions begin to soften, 3 to 4 minutes. 2. Transfer the mixture to the insert of a 5- to 7-quart crock pot. Add the remaining ingredients and stir to combine. Cover and cook on low for 4 to 5 hours, until the cabbage is tender. 3. Serve the sauerkraut from the cooker set on warm.

Black Bean Potato au Gratin

Prep time: 25 minutes | Cook time: 8 hours | Serves 6

- 2 (15-ounce / 425-g) cans black beans, rinsed and drained
- 1 (10¾-ounce / 305-g) can condensed cream of mushroom soup, undiluted
- 1 medium sweet red pepper, chopped
- 1 cup frozen peas
- 1 cup chopped sweet onion
- 1 celery rib, thinly sliced
- 2 garlic cloves, minced
- 1 teaspoon dried thyme
- ¼ teaspoon coarsely ground pepper
- 1½ pounds (680 g) medium red potatoes, cut into ¼-inch slices
- 1 teaspoon salt
- 1 cup shredded cheddar cheese

1. In a large bowl, combine the beans, soup, red pepper, peas, onion, celery, garlic, thyme and pepper. Spoon half of mixture into a greased 3- or 4-quart crock pot. Layer with half of the potatoes, salt and cheese. Repeat layers. Cover and cook on low for 8 to 10 hours or until potatoes are tender.

Wine-Braised Artichokes

Prep time: 15 minutes | Cook time: 4½ to 5 hours | Serves 6

- 2 large lemons, cut into quarters
- 2 bay leaves
- 1 teaspoon dried thyme
- 2 cups dry white wine or vermouth
- 10 black peppercorns
- 6 cloves garlic, peeled
- 6 large globe artichokes, tough outer leaves peeled away, stems trimmed flush with the bottom

1. Squeeze the lemons into the insert of a 5- to 7-quart crock pot. Add the lemon rinds, bay leaves, thyme, wine, peppercorns, and garlic. 2. Arrange the artichokes stem-side down in the crock pot insert. Cover and cook on low for 4½ to 5 hours, until the leaves release easily and the heart is tender when pierced with the tip of a sharp knife. 3. Remove the artichoke hearts from the cooker and serve hot or at room temperature.

Potatoes Boulangerie

Prep time: 20 minutes | Cook time: 2½ to 3 hours | Serves 6 to 8

- 6 medium russet potatoes, peeled and cut into ¼-inch-thick slices
- 6 strips bacon, cut into ½-inch pieces
- 3 leeks, thinly sliced, using the white and some of the
- tender green parts
- 2 teaspoons dried thyme
- 1 cup double-strength chicken broth
- 1½ teaspoons salt
- 1 teaspoon Tabasco sauce
- 1 cup heavy cream

1. Coat the insert of a 5- to 7-quart crock pot with nonstick cooking spray or line it with a crock pot liner according to the manufacturer's directions. Arrange the potatoes in the cooker and set aside. 2. Cook the bacon in a large skillet until crisp, then transfer to paper towels to drain. Cook the leeks and thyme in the bacon drippings until the leeks are soft, 2 to 3 minutes. 3. Add the chicken broth, salt, and Tabasco to the skillet and heat, scraping up any browned bits from the bot tom of the pan. Pour the contents of the skillet over the potatoes and pour the heavy cream evenly over the potatoes. Cover and cook on high for 2½ to 3 hours, until the potatoes are tender. 4. Serve from the crock pot set on warm.

Crock pot Caponata

Prep time: 15 minutes | Cook time: 5½ hours | Serves 6 to 8

- 1 pound (454 g) plum tomatoes, chopped
- 1 eggplant, not peeled, cut into ½-inch pieces
- 2 medium zucchini, cut into ½-inch pieces
- 1 large yellow onion, finely chopped
- 3 stalks celery, sliced
- ½ cup chopped fresh parsley
- 2 tablespoons red wine
- vinegar
- 1 tablespoon brown sugar
- ¼ cup raisins
- ¼ cup tomato paste
- 1 teaspoon sea salt
- ¼ teaspoon black pepper
- ¼ cup pine nuts
- 2 tablespoons capers, drained
- 3 tablespoons oil-cured black olives (optional)

1. Combine the tomatoes, eggplant, zucchini, onion, celery, and parsley in the crock pot. Add the vinegar, brown sugar, raisins, and tomato paste. Sprinkle with the salt and pepper. 2. Cover and cook on low for 5½ hours, or until thoroughly cooked. 3. Stir in the pine nuts and capers, and olives (if using). Serve hot.

Mom's Buttered and Parsleyed Potatoes

Prep time: 15 minutes | Cook time: 4 to 5 hours | Serves 6

- 2½ pounds (1.1 kg) fingerling potatoes, scrubbed and cut in half
- ½ cup (1 stick) unsalted butter, melted
- ¼ cup olive oil
- 6 fresh sage leaves, finely chopped
- 1½ teaspoons salt
- ½ teaspoon freshly ground black pepper
- ¼ cup finely chopped fresh Italian parsley, for garnish
- ¼ cup freshly grated Parmesan cheese, for garnish

1. Put the potatoes in the insert of a 5- to 7-quart crock pot. Add the butter, oil, sage, salt, and pepper and stir to distribute the ingredients. Cover and cook on low for 4 to 5 hours, until the potatoes are tender. 2. Combine the parsley and cheese in a small bowl and sprinkle over the top of the potatoes. 3. Serve the potatoes immediately.

Greek-Style Green Beans

Prep time: 5 minutes | Cook time: 2 to 5 hours | Serves 6

- 20 ounces (567 g) whole or cut-up frozen green beans (not French cut)
- 2 cups tomato sauce
- 2 teaspoons dried onion
- flakes (optional)
- Pinch of dried marjoram or oregano
- Pinch of ground nutmeg
- Pinch of cinnamon

1. Combine all ingredients in crock pot, mixing together thoroughly. 2. Cover and cook on low 2 to 4 hours if the beans are defrosted, or 3 to 5 hours on low if the beans are frozen, or until the beans are done to your liking.

Braised Root Vegetables

Prep time: 30 minutes | Cook time: 2½ to 5 hours | Serves 6 to 8

- 2 medium sweet potatoes, peeled and cut into ½-inch pieces
- 3 medium carrots, peeled and cut into ½-inch pieces
- 2 medium parsnips, peeled and cut into ½-inch pieces
- 2 medium red or Yukon gold potatoes, scrubbed and cut into ½-inch pieces
- 2 cups ½-inch pieces peeled and seeded butternut
- squash
- 2 medium red onions, quartered and separated
- ½ cup (1 stick) unsalted butter, melted
- ½ cup chicken or vegetable broth
- 1 teaspoon dried thyme
- 2 teaspoons salt
- 1 teaspoon freshly ground black pepper

1. Stir together all the ingredients in the insert of a 5- to 7-quart

crock pot. Cover and cook on high 2½ to 3 hours or on low for 4 to 5 hours. 2. Remove the vegetables from the crock pot with a slotted spoon and arrange on a serving platter. Spoon some of the sauce over the vegetables and serve.

Glazed Sweet Potatoes

Prep time: 20 minutes | Cook time: 3 to 4 hours | Serves 8 to 10

- 8 to 10 medium sweet potatoes
- ½ teaspoon salt
- ¾ cup brown sugar
- 2 tablespoons butter
- 1 tablespoon flour
- ¼ cup water

1. Cook sweet potatoes in 2 to 3 inches water in a large saucepan until barely soft. Drain. When cool enough to handle, peel and slice into crock pot. 2. While potatoes are cooking in the saucepan, combine remaining ingredients in a microwave-safe bowl. 3. Microwave on high for 1½ minutes. Stir. Repeat until glaze thickens slightly. 4. Pour glaze over peeled, cooked sweet potatoes in crock pot. 5. Cover and cook on high 3 to 4 hours.

"Baked" Acorn Squash

Prep time: 15 minutes | Cook time: 5 to 6 hours | Serves 4

- 2 acorn squash
- ⅔ cup cracker crumbs
- ½ cup coarsely chopped pecans
- ⅓ cup butter, melted
- 4 tablespoons brown sugar
- ½ teaspoon salt
- ¼ teaspoon ground nutmeg
- 2 tablespoons orange juice

1. Cut squash in half. Remove seeds. 2. Combine remaining ingredients. Spoon into squash halves. Place squash in crock pot. 3. Cover. Cook on low 5 to 6 hours, or until squash is tender.

Sweet Potato Casserole

Prep time: 10 minutes | Cook time: 3 to 4 hours | Serves 8

- 2 (29-ounce / 822-g) cans sweet potatoes, drained and mashed
- 2 tablespoons brown sugar
- 1 tablespoon orange juice
- 2 eggs, beaten
- ½ cup fat-free milk
- ⅓ cup chopped pecans
- ⅓ cup brown sugar
- 2 tablespoons flour
- 2 teaspoons butter, melted

1. Combine sweet potatoes and 2 tablespoons brown sugar. 2. Stir in orange juice, eggs, and milk. Transfer to greased crock pot. 3. Combine pecans, ⅓ cup brown sugar, flour, and butter. Spread over sweet potatoes. 4. Cover. Cook on high 3 to 4 hours.

Balsamic Root Vegetables

Prep time: 20 minutes | Cook time: 4 to 5 hours | Serves 6 to 8

- Nonstick cooking oil spray
- 1 pound (454 g) parsnips, peeled and cut into 1½-inch cubes
- 1 pound (454 g) carrots, peeled and cut into 1½-inch pieces
- 2 large red onions, coarsely chopped
- ¾ cup dried apricots or figs
- 1½ pounds (680 g) sweet potatoes, peeled and cut into 1½-inch cubes
- 1 tablespoon light brown sugar
- 3 tablespoons olive oil
- 2 tablespoons balsamic vinegar
- 1 teaspoon sea salt
- ½ teaspoon black pepper
- ⅓ cup chopped fresh flat-leaf parsley

1. Coat the interior of the crock pot crock with nonstick cooking oil spray. 2. Add the parsnips, carrots, onions, and apricots in the prepared crock pot crock, and layer the sweet potatoes over the top. 3. Whisk together the brown sugar, olive oil, balsamic vinegar, salt, and pepper in a small bowl. Pour over vegetable mixture, but do not stir. 4. Cover and cook on high for 4 to 5 hours, or until the vegetables are tender. Toss with parsley just before serving hot.

Refrigerator Mashed Potatoes

Prep time: 30 minutes | Cook time: 2 hours | Serves 8 to 10

- 5 pounds (2.3 kg) potatoes
- 1 (8-ounce / 227-g) package cream cheese, softened
- 1 cup sour cream
- 1 teaspoon salt
- ¼ teaspoon pepper
- ¼ cup crisp bacon, crumbled
- 2 tablespoons butter

1. Cook and mash potatoes. 2. Add remaining ingredients except butter. Put in crock pot. Dot with butter. 3. Cover. Cook on low 2 hours.

Creamy Broccoli Casserole

Prep time: 15 minutes | Cook time: 6 hours | Serves 6

- 1 tablespoon extra-virgin olive oil
- 1 pound (454 g) broccoli, cut into florets
- 1 pound (454 g) cauliflower, cut into florets
- ¼ cup almond flour
- 2 cups coconut milk
- ½ teaspoon ground nutmeg
- Pinch freshly ground black pepper
- 1½ cups shredded Gouda cheese, divided

1. Lightly grease the insert of the crock pot with the olive oil. 2. Place the broccoli and cauliflower in the insert. 3. In a small bowl, stir together the almond flour, coconut milk, nutmeg, pepper, and 1 cup of the cheese. 4. Pour the coconut milk mixture over the vegetables and top the casserole with the remaining ½ cup of the cheese. 5. Cover and cook on low for 6 hours. 6. Serve warm.

Glazed Brussels Sprouts with Pine Nuts

Prep time: 10 minutes | Cook time: 2 to 3 hours | Serves 4 to 6

- 1 cup balsamic vinegar
- ¼ cup honey
- 2 pounds (907 g) Brussels sprouts, trimmed and halved
- 2 cups vegetable stock
- 1 teaspoon sea salt
- Black pepper
- 2 tablespoons extra-virgin olive oil
- ¼ cup pine nuts, toasted
- ¼ cup grated Parmesan cheese

1. Mix the balsamic vinegar and honey in a small saucepan over medium-high heat. Stir constantly until the sugar has dissolved. Bring to a boil, reduce the heat to low, and simmer until the glaze is reduced by half, about 20 minutes. The glaze is finished when it will coat the back of a spoon. Set aside. 2. 2 Combine the Brussels sprouts, stock, and ½ teaspoon salt in the crock pot. Cover and cook on high for 2 to 3 hours, or until the Brussels sprouts are tender. 3. Drain the Brussels sprouts and transfer to a serving dish. Season with salt and pepper. Drizzle with 2 tablespoons or more of the balsamic glaze and the olive oil, then sprinkle with the pine nuts and Parmesan. Serve hot.

Hash Brown Casserole

Prep time: 15 minutes | Cook time: 4 hours | Serves 8

- Cooking spray or 1 tablespoon extra-virgin olive oil
- 1 medium onion, finely chopped
- 3 garlic cloves, minced
- 1 (32-ounce / 907-g) bag frozen hash brown potatoes, thawed
- 3 cups shredded sharp Cheddar cheese
- 2 cups sour cream
- 1¼ cups low-sodium chicken stock
- ½ cup heavy (whipping) cream
- ¾ teaspoon kosher salt, plus more for seasoning
- ½ teaspoon freshly ground black pepper
- ½ teaspoon onion powder

1. Use the cooking spray or olive oil to coat the inside (bottom and sides) of the crock pot. In a large bowl, combine the onion, garlic, hash browns, Cheddar, sour cream, chicken stock, heavy cream, salt, pepper, and onion powder. Stir until thoroughly mixed. Add the mixture to the crock pot. Cover and cook on high for 1½ hours. Reduce the heat to low and cook for another 2½ hours. 2. Season with additional salt, if needed. Let the casserole sit for 10 minutes before serving.

Squash Casserole

Prep time: 15 minutes | Cook time: 7 to 9 hours | Serves 4 to 6

- 2 pounds (907 g) yellow summer squash or zucchini thinly sliced (about 6 cups)
- Half a medium onion, chopped
- 1 cup peeled, shredded carrot
- 1 (10¾-ounce / 305-g)
- can condensed cream of chicken soup
- 1 cup sour cream
- ¼ cup flour
- 1 (8-ounce / 227-g) package seasoned stuffing crumbs
- ½ cup butter, melted

1. Combine squash, onion, carrots, and soup. 2. Mix together sour cream and flour. Stir into vegetables. 3. Toss stuffing crumbs with butter. Spread half in bottom of crock pot. Add vegetable mixture. Top with remaining crumbs. 4. Cover. Cook on low 7 to 9 hours.

"Baked" Corn

Prep time: 5 minutes | Cook time: 3 hours | Serves 8

- 1 quart corn (be sure to thaw and drain if using frozen corn)
- 2 eggs, beaten
- 1 teaspoon salt
- 1 cup fat-free milk
- ⅛ teaspoon black pepper
- 2 teaspoons oil
- 2 tablespoons sugar
- 3 tablespoons flour

1. Combine all ingredients well. Pour into crock pot sprayed with fat-free cooking spray. 2. Cover. Cook on high 3 hours.

Cheesy Scalloped Potatoes

Prep time: 15 minutes | Cook time: 3 to 4 hours | Serves 8 to 10

- 2 tablespoons dried minced onion
- 1 medium clove garlic, minced
- 1 teaspoon salt
- 8 to 10 medium fresh potatoes, sliced, divided
- 1 (8-ounce / 227-g) package cream cheese, cubed, divided
- ½ cup shredded Cheddar cheese (optional)
- Nonstick cooking spray

1. Spray interior of crock pot with nonstick cooking spray. 2. In a small bowl, combine onion, garlic, and salt. 3. Layer about one-fourth of the potatoes into the crock pot. 4. Sprinkle one-fourth of onion-garlic mixture over potatoes. 5. Spoon about one-third of cream cheese cubes over top. 6. Repeat layers, ending with the seasoning. 7. Cook on high 3 to 4 hours, or until potatoes are tender. 8. Stir potatoes to spread out the cream cheese. If you wish, you can mash the potatoes at this point. 9. If you like, sprinkle shredded cheese over top of the sliced or mashed potatoes. 10. Cover and cook an additional 10 minutes, or until the cheese is melted.

Super Green Beans

Prep time: 15 minutes | Cook time: 1 to 2 hours | Serves 5

- 2 (14½-ounce / 411-g) cans green beans, undrained
- 1 cup cooked cubed ham
- ⅓ cup finely chopped onion
- 1 tablespoon butter, melted, or bacon drippings

1. Place undrained beans in cooker. Add remaining ingredients and mix well. 2. Cook on high 1 to 2 hours, or until steaming hot.

Apple Stuffing

Prep time: 20 minutes | Cook time: 4 to 5 hours | Serves 4 to 5

- 1 stick (½ cup) butter, divided
- 1 cup chopped walnuts
- 2 onions, chopped
- 1 (14-ounce / 397-g)
- package dry herb-seasoned stuffing mix
- 1½ cups applesauce
- Water (optional)
- Nonstick cooking spray

1. In nonstick skillet, melt 2 tablespoons of butter. Sauté walnuts over medium heat until toasted, about 5 minutes, stirring frequently. Remove from skillet and set aside. 2. Melt remaining butter in skillet. Add onions and cook 3 to 4 minutes, or until almost tender. Set aside. 3. Spray crock pot with nonstick cooking spray. Place dry stuffing mix in crock pot. 4. Add onion-butter mixture and stir. Add applesauce and stir. 5. Cover and cook on low 4 to 5 hours, or until heated through. Check after Stuffing has cooked for 3½ hours. If it's sticking to the cooker, drying out, or becoming too brown on the edges, stir in ½ to 1 cup water. Continue cooking. 6. Sprinkle with walnuts before serving.

Sweet Potatoes and Apples

Prep time: 15 minutes | Cook time: 6 to 8 hours | Serves 8 to 10

- 3 large sweet potatoes, peeled and cubed
- 3 large tart and firm apples, peeled and sliced
- ½ to ¾ teaspoon salt
- ⅛ to ¼ teaspoon pepper
- 1 teaspoon sage
- 1 teaspoon ground cinnamon
- 4 tablespoons (½ stick) butter, melted
- ¼ cup maple syrup
- Toasted sliced almonds or chopped pecans (optional)

1. Place half the sweet potatoes in crock pot. Layer in half the apple slices. 2. Mix together seasonings. Sprinkle half over apples. 3. Mix together butter and maple syrup. Spoon half over seasonings. 4. Repeat layers. 5. Cover. Cook on low 6 to 8 hours or until potatoes are soft, stirring occasionally. 6. To add a bit of crunch, sprinkle with toasted almonds or pecans when serving. 7. Serve.

Crock-Baked Sweets

Prep time: 5 minutes | Cook time: 6 hours | Serves 6 to 8

- 6 to 8 medium sweet potatoes, scrubbed

1. Prick each potato a few times with the tip of a sharp paring knife. Arrange the potatoes in the insert of a 5- to 7-quart crock pot. Cover and cook on low for 6 hours, until the potatoes are tender when pierced with the tip of a knife. 2. Serve the potatoes split open.

Potluck Candied Sweet Potatoes

Prep time: 20 minutes | Cook time: 5 hours | Serves 12

- 1 cup packed brown sugar
- 1 cup sugar
- 8 medium sweet potatoes, peeled and cut into ½-inch slices
- ¼ cup butter, melted
- 2 teaspoons vanilla extract
- ¼ teaspoon salt
- 2 tablespoons cornstarch
- 2 tablespoons cold water
- Minced fresh parsley (optional)

1. In a small bowl, combine sugars. In a greased 5-quart crock pot, layer a third of the sweet potatoes; sprinkle with a third of the sugar mixture. Repeat layers twice. In a small bowl, combine the butter, vanilla and salt; drizzle over potatoes. Cover and cook on low for 5 to 6 hours or until sweet potatoes are tender. 2. Using a slotted spoon, transfer potatoes to a serving dish; keep warm. Pour cooking juices into a small saucepan; bring to a boil. In a small bowl, combine cornstarch and water until smooth; stir into pan. Return to a boil, stirring constantly; cook and stir for 1 to 2 minutes or until thickened. Spoon over sweet potatoes. 3. Sprinkle with parsley if desired.

Greek Stuffed Peppers

Prep time: 20 minutes | Cook time: 4 hours | Serves 4

- 4 large bell peppers, any color
- 1 (15-ounce / 425-g) can cannellini beans, rinsed and drained
- 1 cup crumbled feta cheese
- ½ cup uncooked couscous
- 4 green onions, white and green parts separated,
- thinly sliced
- 1 garlic clove, minced
- 1 teaspoon oregano
- Coarse sea salt
- Freshly ground black pepper
- 1 lemon, cut into 4 wedges, for serving

1. Slice a very thin layer from the base of each bell pepper so they sit upright. Slice off the tops just below stem and discard the stem only. Chop the remaining top portions, and place in a medium bowl. With a spoon, scoop out the ribs and seeds from the peppers. 2. Add the beans, feta, couscous, white parts of the green onions, garlic, and oregano to a medium bowl.

Season with salt and pepper and toss to combine. 3. Stuff the peppers with bean mixture, and place them upright in the crock pot. Cover and cook on high for 4 hours, or until the peppers are tender and the couscous is cooked. 4. To serve, sprinkle the peppers with the green parts of the green onions and plate with 1 lemon wedge alongside each pepper.

Cheesy Creamed Corn with Bacon

Prep time: 15 minutes | Cook time: 3 hours | Serves 8

- 12 ears of corn, shucked and cut from the cob, or 2 pounds (907 g) frozen corn kernels
- 2 bacon slices, finely chopped
- 8 ounces (227 g) cream cheese, at room temperature
- 6 ounces (170 g) American
- cheese, finely diced
- ½ cup whole milk
- 3 ounces (85 g) sour cream
- 3 fresh thyme sprigs
- 2 bay leaves
- ¾ teaspoon kosher salt, plus more for seasoning
- ½ teaspoon freshly ground black pepper, plus more for seasoning

1. In the crock pot, combine the corn, bacon, cream cheese, cheese, milk, sour cream, thyme, and bay leaves. Season with the salt and pepper, and stir to combine. Cover and cook on low for 3 hours, until the corn is cooked and the sauce has thickened slightly. 2. Remove the cover and discard the thyme and bay leaves. Season with additional salt and pepper as needed, and serve.

Sweet-Braised Red Cabbage

Prep time: 15 minutes | Cook time: 7 to 8 hours | Serves 8

- 1 tablespoon extra-virgin olive oil
- 1 small red cabbage, coarsely shredded (about 6 cups)
- ½ sweet onion, thinly sliced
- ¼ cup apple cider vinegar
- 3 tablespoons granulated erythritol
- 2 teaspoons minced garlic
- ½ teaspoon ground nutmeg
- ⅛ teaspoon ground cloves
- 2 tablespoons butter
- Salt, for seasoning
- Freshly ground black pepper, for seasoning
- ½ cup chopped walnuts, for garnish
- ½ cup crumbled blue cheese, for garnish
- Pink peppercorns, for garnish (optional)

1. Lightly grease the insert of the crock pot with the olive oil. 2. Add the cabbage, onion, apple cider vinegar, erythritol, garlic, nutmeg, and cloves to the insert, stirring to mix well. 3. Break off little slices of butter and scatter them on top of the cabbage mixture. 4. Cover and cook on low for 7 to 8 hours. 5. Season with salt and pepper. 6. Serve topped with the walnuts, blue cheese, and peppercorns (if desired).

Cheddar Creamed Corn

Prep time: 10 minutes | Cook time: 3 hours | Serves 9

- 2 (one 16-ounce / 454-g, one 12-ounce / 340-g) packages frozen corn, thawed
- 1 (8-ounce / 227-g) package cream cheese, cubed
- ¾ cup shredded cheddar cheese
- ¼ cup butter, melted
- ¼ cup heavy whipping cream
- ½ teaspoon salt
- ¼ teaspoon pepper

1. In a 3- or 4-quart crock pot, combine all ingredients. Cook, covered, on low 3 to 3½ hours or until cheese is melted and corn is tender. Stir just before serving.

Simple Spaghetti Squash

Prep time: 15 minutes | Cook time: 6 hours | Serves 8

- 1 small spaghetti squash, washed
- ½ cup chicken stock
- ¼ cup butter
- Salt, for seasoning
- Freshly ground black pepper, for seasoning

1. Place the squash and chicken stock in the insert of the crock pot. The squash should not touch the sides of the insert. 2. Cook on low for 6 hours. 3. Let the squash cool for 10 minutes and cut in half. 4. Scrape out the squash strands into a bowl with a fork. When finished, add the butter and toss to combine. 5. Season with salt and pepper and serve.

Creamed Kale

Prep time: 20 minutes | Cook time: 3 hours | Serves 8

- Cooking spray or 1 tablespoon extra-virgin olive oil
- ½ stick unsalted butter
- 2 garlic cloves, minced
- ½ cup heavy (whipping) cream
- 2 ounces (57 g) cream cheese
- 1½ cups whole milk
- 1 cup low-sodium chicken stock
- 4 tablespoons all-purpose
- flour
- ½ cup finely grated Parmesan cheese
- ½ teaspoon kosher salt, plus more for seasoning
- ½ teaspoon freshly ground black pepper, plus more for seasoning
- ¼ teaspoon ground nutmeg
- ¼ teaspoon red pepper flakes
- 2 bunches kale, washed, stemmed, and leaves torn

1. If using a crock pot with a stove-top function to make the sauce, first use the cooking spray or olive oil to coat the inside (bottom and sides) of the crock pot. In the crock pot or in a Dutch oven or heavy-bottomed pan over medium-high heat, prepare the sauce by whisking together the butter, garlic, whipping cream, cream cheese, milk, chicken stock, flour, and Parmesan until the butter and cheese are melted and the flour is incorporated, and the sauce is free of lumps. 2. If you prepared the sauce outside the crock pot, use the cooking spray or olive oil to coat the inside (bottom and sides) of the crock pot. Add the sauce to the crock pot, along with the salt, pepper, nutmeg, red pepper flakes, and kale. Stir to combine. Cover and cook on low for 3 hours. 3. Season with additional salt and pepper, as needed. Serve.

Fruity Sweet Potatoes

Prep time: 15 minutes | Cook time: 6 to 8 hours | Serves 6

- 2 pounds (907 g) sweet potatoes or yams
- 1½ cups applesauce
- ⅔ cup brown sugar
- 3 tablespoons butter, melted
- 1 teaspoon cinnamon
- Chopped nuts (optional)

1. Peel sweet potatoes if you wish. Cut into cubes or slices. Place in crock pot. 2. In a bowl, mix together applesauce, brown sugar, butter, and cinnamon. Spoon over potatoes. 3. Cover and cook on low 6 to 8 hours, or until potatoes are tender. 4. Mash potatoes and sauce together if you wish with a large spoon—or spoon potatoes into serving dish and top with the sauce. 5. Sprinkle with nuts, if you want.

Dried Corn

Prep time: 5 minutes | Cook time: 4 hours | Serves 4

- 1 (15-ounce / 425-g) can dried corn
- 2 tablespoons sugar
- 3 tablespoons butter,
- softened
- 1 teaspoon salt
- 1 cup half-and-half
- 2 tablespoons water

1. Place all ingredients in crock pot. Mix together well. 2. Cover and cook on low 4 hours. 3. Serve.

Bavarian Cabbage

Prep time: 10 minutes | Cook time: 3 to 8 hours | Serves 4 to 8

- 1 small head red cabbage, sliced
- 1 medium onion, chopped
- 3 tart apples, cored and quartered
- 2 teaspoons salt
- 1 cup hot water
- 2 tablespoons sugar
- ⅓ cup vinegar
- 3 tablespoons bacon drippings

1. Place all ingredients in crock pot in order listed. 2. Cover. Cook on low 8 hours, or on high 3 hours. Stir well before serving.

Kale with Bacon

Prep time: 15 minutes | Cook time: 6 hours | Serves 8

- 2 tablespoons bacon fat
- 2 pounds (907 g) kale, rinsed and chopped roughly
- 12 bacon slices, cooked and chopped
- 2 teaspoons minced garlic
- 2 cups vegetable broth
- Salt, for seasoning
- Freshly ground black pepper, for seasoning

1. Generously grease the insert of the crock pot with the bacon fat. 2. Add the kale, bacon, garlic, and broth to the insert. Gently toss to mix. 3. Cover and cook on low for 6 hours. 4. Season with salt and pepper, and serve hot.

Simply Sweet Potatoes

Prep time: 5 minutes | Cook time: 6 to 9 hours | Serves 4

- 3 large sweet potatoes
- ¼ cup water

1. Place unpeeled sweet potatoes into crock pot. 2. Add ¼ cup water. 3. Cover and cook on high 1 hour. Then turn to low and cook for 5 to 8 hours, or until potatoes are tender.

Green Beans with Cipollini Onions and Cremini Mushrooms

Prep time: 15 minutes | Cook time: 4 to 5 hours | Serves 6 to 8

- ½ cup (1 stick) unsalted butter, melted
- ¼ cup soy sauce
- 2 tablespoons rice wine (mirin) or dry sherry
- 2 cloves garlic, minced
- 24 cipollini onions, peeled
- 8 ounces (227 g) cremini mushrooms, quartered
- 2 pounds (907 g) green beans, ends trimmed, cut into 1-inch lengths

1. Combine the butter, soy sauce, rice wine, and garlic into the insert of a 5- to 7-quart crock pot and stir to blend. 2. Add the remaining ingredients and toss to coat with the butter mixture. Cover and cook on low for 4 to 5 hours, until the beans and onions are tender. 3. Drain the liquid from the vegetables and serve the vegetables immediately.

Rosy Sweet Potatoes

Prep time: 5 minutes | Cook time: 3 to 4 hours | Serves 8

- 1 (40-ounce / 1.1-kg) can unsweetened sweet potato chunks, drained
- 1 (21-ounce / 595-g) can lite apple pie filling
- ⅓ cup brown sugar
- ⅓ cup red hots
- 1 teaspoon ground cinnamon
- Nonfat cooking spray

1. Combine all ingredients in a large bowl. Pour into crock pot sprayed with nonfat cooking spray. 2. Cover. Cook on low 3 to 4 hours.

South-of-the-Border Stewed Tomatoes

Prep time: 15 minutes | Cook time: 8 hours | Serves 6

- 2 tablespoons olive oil
- 1 medium onion, coarsely chopped
- 2 Anaheim chiles, seeded and coarsely chopped
- 1 teaspoon ground cumin
- 1 teaspoon dried oregano
- 2 tablespoons sugar
- 1½ teaspoons salt
- 10 large tomatoes, peeled, cored, and cut into wedges

1. Heat the oil in a large skillet over medium-high heat. Add the onion, chiles, cumin, and oregano and sauté until the onion begins to soften, 4 to 5 minutes. 2. Transfer the mixture to the insert of a 5- to 7-quart crock pot and stir in the sugar, salt, and tomatoes. Cover and cook on low for 8 hours. 3. Allow the tomatoes to cool before serving.

Pineapple Sweet Potatoes

Prep time: 5 minutes | Cook time: 2 to 4 hours | Serves 10

- 1 (10-ounce / 283-g) can unsweetened crushed pineapple, drained
- 2 tablespoons dark brown
- sugar
- 1 (40-ounce / 1.1-kg) can unsweetened yams, drained
- Cooking spray

1. Mix crushed pineapples with brown sugar. 2. Combine with yams in crock pot sprayed with cooking spray. 3. Cover. Cook on low 2 to 4 hours, or until heated through.

Quick Broccoli Fix

Prep time: 15 minutes | Cook time: 5 to 6 hours | Serves 6

- 1 pound (454 g) fresh or frozen broccoli, cut up
- 1 (10¾-ounce / 305-g) can cream of mushroom soup
- ½ cup mayonnaise
- ½ cup plain yogurt
- ½ pound (227 g) sliced
- fresh mushrooms
- 1 cup shredded Cheddar cheese, divided
- 1 cup crushed saltine crackers
- Sliced almonds (optional)

1. Microwave broccoli for 3 minutes. Place in greased crock pot. 2. Combine soup, mayonnaise, yogurt, mushrooms, and ½ cup cheese. Pour over broccoli. 3. Cover. Cook on low 5 to 6 hours. 4. Top with remaining cheese and crackers for last half hour of cooking time. 5. Top with sliced almonds, for a special touch, before serving.

Chapter 8
Snacks and Appetizers

Hearty Beef Dip Fondue

Prep time: 20 minutes | Cook time: 6 hours | Makes 2½ cups

- 1¾ cups milk
- 2 (8-ounce / 227-g) packages cream cheese, cubed
- 2 teaspoons dry mustard
- ¼ cup chopped green onions
- 2½ ounces (71 g) sliced dried beef, shredded or torn into small pieces
- French bread, cut into bite-sized pieces, each having a side of crust

1. Heat milk in crock pot on high. 2. Add cheese. Stir until melted. 3. Add mustard, green onions, and dried beef. Stir well. 4. Cover. Cook on low for up to 6 hours. 5. Serve by dipping bread pieces on long forks into mixture.

Maytag Blue and Walnut Dip with Apple Dippers

Prep time: 10 minutes | Cook time: 2 to 3 hours | Serves 8

- 2 (8-ounce / 227-g) packages cream cheese at room temperature
- ½ cup mayonnaise
- 2 tablespoons Ruby Port
- 6 drops Tabasco sauce
- 1 cup chopped walnuts
- 2 cups crumbled Maytag blue cheese
- 4 to 6 Granny Smith Apples, cored and cut into 8 wedges each, for serving
- Crackers for serving

1. Coat the insert of a 1½- to 3-quart crock pot with nonstick cooking spray. Put the cream cheese, mayonnaise, port, Tabasco, walnuts, and blue cheese in a mixing bowl and stir until blended. 2. Transfer the mixture to the crock pot insert. Cover and cook on low for 2 to 3 hours, until heated through and bubbly. 3. Serve from the cooker set on warm with the apple wedges and crackers.

Everyone's Favorite Snack Mix

Prep time: 20 minutes | Cook time: 2 hours | Serves 8 to 10

- ½ cup (2 sticks) unsalted butter, melted
- 2 tablespoons Lawry's seasoned salt
- 1 tablespoon garlic salt
- ¼ cup Worcestershire sauce
- 6 shakes Tabasco sauce
- 4 cups Crispix cereal
- 2 cups mixed nuts
- 1 (8- to 10-ounce / 227- to 283-g) bag pretzel sticks
- 1 (5-ounce / 142-g) bag plain or Parmesan goldfish crackers
- 2 (3-ounce / 85-g) bags herbed croutons

1. Combine the butter, seasoned salt, garlic salt, Worcestershire, and Tabasco in the insert of a 5- to 7-quart crock pot and stir to blend. Add the remaining ingredients and gently stir to coat each piece with the flavored butter. 2. Cook uncovered on high for 2 hours, stirring occasionally. Reduce the heat to low and cook for an additional hour, stirring every 15 minutes, until the mix is dry and crisp. 3. Transfer to baking sheets to cool completely before serving, or store in airtight containers.

Apple Kielbasa

Prep time: 15 minutes | Cook time: 6 to 8 hours | Serves 12

- 2 pounds (907 g) fully cooked kielbasa sausage, cut into 1-inch pieces
- ¾ cup brown sugar
- 1 cup chunky applesauce
- 2 cloves garlic, minced

1. Combine all ingredients in crock pot. 2. Cover and cook on low 6 to 8 hours until thoroughly heated.

crock pot Candy

Prep time: 10 minutes | Cook time: 2 hours | Makes 80 to 100 pieces

- 1½ pounds (680 g) almond bark, broken
- 1 (4-ounce / 113-g) Baker's Brand German sweet chocolate bar, broken
- 8 ounces (227 g) chocolate chips
- 8 ounces (227 g) peanut butter chips
- 2 pounds (907 g) lightly salted or unsalted peanuts

1. Spray inside of cooker with nonstick cooking spray. 2. Layer ingredients into crock pot in the order given above. 3. Cook on low 2 hours. Do not stir or lift the lid during the cooking time. 4. After 2 hours, mix well. 5. Drop by teaspoonfuls onto waxed paper. Refrigerate for approximately 45 minutes before serving or storing.

Warm Clam Dip

Prep time: 15 minutes | Cook time: 2 to 3 hours | Serves 6 to 8

- 2 (8-ounce / 227-g) packages cream cheese at room temperature and cut into cubes
- ½ cup mayonnaise
- 3 green onions, finely chopped, using the white and tender green parts
- 2 cloves garlic, minced
- 3 (8-ounce / 227-g) cans minced or chopped clams, drained with ¼ cup clam juice reserved
- 1 tablespoon Worcestershire sauce
- 2 teaspoons anchovy paste
- ¼ cup finely chopped fresh Italian parsley

1. Coat the insert of a 1½- to 3-quart crock pot with nonstick cooking spray. Combine all the ingredients in a large mixing bowl, adding the clam juice to thin the dip. 2. Transfer the mixture to the crock pot, cover, and cook on low for 2 to 3 hours, until bubbling. 3. Serve from the cooker set on warm.

Kielbasa in Spicy Barbecue Sauce

Prep time: 20 minutes | Cook time: 4 to 5 hours | Serves 8

- 2 cups ketchup
- ½ cup firmly packed light brown sugar
- 1 tablespoon Worcestershire sauce
- 1 teaspoon Creole mustard
- 1 teaspoon hot sauce
- 1 medium onion, finely chopped
- ½ cup bourbon
- 2 pounds (907 g) kielbasa or other smoked sausages, cut into ½-inch rounds

1. Combine all the ingredients in the insert of a 3- to 5-quart crock pot. Cover and cook on low for 4 to 5 hours, until the sausage is heated through. 2. Serve the kielbasa from the cooker set on warm, with 6-inch skewers.

Little Smokeys in Barbecue Sauce

Prep time: 15 minutes | Cook time: 2 to 3 hours | Serves 6 to 8

- 2 (16-ounce / 454-g) packages mini smoked sausages (Hillshire Farms is a reliable brand)
- 2 tablespoons canola or vegetable oil
- 1 medium onion, finely chopped
- 2 teaspoons ancho chile
- powder
- 1½ cups ketchup
- 1 (8-ounce / 227-g) can tomato sauce
- ¼ cup molasses
- 2 tablespoons Worcestershire sauce
- ¼ cup honey

1. Arrange the sausages in the insert of a 1½- to 3-quart crock pot. Heat the oil in a small skillet over medium-high heat. Add the onion and chili powder and sauté until the onion is softened, about 3 minutes. 2. Transfer the contents of the skillet to the crock pot insert. Add the ketchup, tomato sauce, molasses, Worcestershire, and honey and stir to blend. Cover and cook over low heat 2 to 3 hours, until the sausages are heated through. 3. Serve the sausages from the cooker set on warm.

Pickled Whiting

Prep time: 10 minutes | Cook time: 3 to 4 hours | Serves 24

- 2 onions, sliced
- 1 cup white vinegar
- ¾ cup Splenda
- 1 teaspoon salt
- 1 tablespoon allspice
- 2 pounds (907 g) frozen individual whiting with skin

1. Combine onions, vinegar, Splenda, salt, and allspice in bottom of crock pot. 2. Slice frozen whiting into 2-inch slices, each with skin on. Place fish in crock pot, pushing it down into the liquid as much as possible. 3. Cook on low 3 to 4 hours.

4. Pour cooking liquid over fish, cover, and refrigerate. Serve when well chilled.

Hot Broccoli Dip

Prep time: 20 minutes | Cook time: 1 hour | Serves 24

- 2 cups fresh or frozen broccoli, chopped
- 4 tablespoons chopped red bell pepper
- 2 (8-ounce / 227-g)
- containers ranch dip
- ½ cup grated Parmesan cheese
- 2 cups shredded Cheddar cheese

1. Mix together all ingredients in your crock pot. 2. Cook on low for 1 hour. 3. Serve.

Pizza Dip

Prep time: 15 minutes | Cook time: 3 to 4 hours | Serves 8

- 2 tablespoons extra-virgin olive oil
- 1 medium onion, finely chopped
- 2 teaspoons dried oregano
- 2 teaspoons dried basil
- Pinch of red pepper flakes
- 3 cloves garlic, minced
- 2 (14- to 15-ounce / 397- to
- 425-g) cans crushed plum tomatoes, with their juice
- 2 tablespoons tomato paste
- 1½ teaspoons salt
- ½ teaspoon freshly ground black pepper
- ½ cup finely chopped fresh Italian parsley

1. Heat the oil in a small saucepan over medium-high heat. Add the onion, oregano, basil, red pepper flakes, and garlic and sauté until the onion is softened, about 3 minutes. 2. Transfer the contents of the skillet to the insert of a 1½- to 3-quart crock pot. Add the remaining ingredients and stir to combine. Cover and cook on low for 3 to 4 hours. 3. Serve from the cooker set on warm.

Garlic Swiss Fondue

Prep time: 10 minutes | Cook time: 2 hours | Makes 3 cups

- 4 cups shredded Swiss cheese
- 1 (10¾-ounce / 305-g) can condensed cheddar cheese soup, undiluted
- 2 tablespoons sherry or chicken broth
- 1 tablespoon Dijon mustard
- 2 garlic cloves, minced
- 2 teaspoons hot pepper sauce
- Cubed French bread baguette
- Sliced apples
- Seedless red grapes

1. In a 1½-quart crock pot, mix the first six ingredients. Cook, covered, on low 2 to 2½ hours or until the cheese is melted, stirring every 30 minutes. Serve warm with bread cubes and fruit.

Snack Mix

Prep time: 10 minutes | Cook time: 2 hours | Serves 10 to 14

- 8 cups Chex cereal, of any combination
- 6 cups pretzels
- 6 tablespoons butter, melted
- 2 tablespoons
- Worcestershire sauce
- 1 teaspoon seasoned salt
- ½ teaspoon garlic powder
- ½ teaspoon onion salt
- ½ teaspoon onion powder

1. Combine first two ingredients in crock pot. 2. Combine butter and seasonings. Pour over dry mixture. Toss until well mixed. 3. Cover. Cook on low 2 hours, stirring every 30 minutes.

Tangy Meatballs

Prep time: 15 minutes | Cook time: 2 to 4 hours | Makes 50 to 60 meatballs

- 2 pounds (907 g) precooked meatballs
- 1 (16-ounce / 454-g) bottle
- barbecue sauce
- 8 ounces (227 g) grape jelly

1. Place meatballs in crock pot. 2. Combine barbecue sauce and jelly in medium-sized mixing bowl. 3. Pour over meatballs and stir well. 4. Cover and cook on high 2 hours, or on low 4 hours. 5. Turn to low and serve.

Refried Bean Dip

Prep time: 20 minutes | Cook time: 2 to 3 hours | Serves 8

- 8 ounces (227 g) spicy sausages, such as chorizo, andouille, or Italian, removed from its casing
- 1 medium onion, chopped
- 2 Anaheim chiles, seeded and chopped
- 1 medium red or yellow bell pepper, seeded and chopped
- 2 (14- to 15-ounce / 397- to
- 425-g) cans refried beans (nonfat are fine here)
- 2 cups finely shredded mild Cheddar cheese, or 1 cup each finely shredded Monterey Jack and sharp Cheddar cheese
- 2 tablespoons finely chopped fresh cilantro
- Tortilla chips for serving

1. Spray the insert of a 1½ - to 3-quart crock pot with nonstick cooking spray. Cook the sausage in a medium skillet over high heat until it is no longer pink, breaking up any large pieces with the side of a spoon. Drain the sausage and put it in a mixing bowl to cool. Add the onion, chiles, and bell pepper to the same skillet and sauté until the bell pepper is softened, about 5 minutes. Add to the bowl with the sausage and allow to cool slightly. Add the refried beans to the bowl and stir to blend. 2. Spoon half the bean mixture into the crock pot insert and sprinkle with half the cheese. Top with the remaining beans

and cheese and sprinkle with the cilantro. Cover and cook on low for 2 to 3 hours. 3. Serve from the cooker set at warm and accompany with sturdy tortilla chips.

Chili Rellanos

Prep time: 15 minutes | Cook time: 6 to 8 hours | Serves 8

- 1¼ cups milk
- 4 eggs, beaten
- 3 tablespoons flour
- 1 (12-ounce / 340-g) can
- chopped green chilies
- 2 cups shredded Cheddar cheese

1. Combine all ingredients in crock pot until well blended. 2. Cover and cook on low for 6 to 8 hours. 3. Serve.

Tangy Cocktail Franks

Prep time: 10 minutes | Cook time: 1 to 2 hours | Serves 12

- 1 (14-ounce / 397-g) jar currant jelly
- ¼ cup prepared mustard
- 3 tablespoons dry sherry
- ¼ teaspoon ground allspice
- 1 (30-ounce / 850-g) can
- unsweetened pineapple chunks
- 1 (6-ounce / 170-g) package low-sodium cocktail franks

1. Melt jelly in crock pot turned on high. Stir in seasonings until blended. 2. Drain pineapple chunks and any liquid in cocktail franks package. Discard juice. Gently stir pineapple and franks into crock pot. 3. Cover. Cook on low 1 to 2 hours. 4. Serve and enjoy.

Barbecued Party Starters

Prep time: 30 minutes | Cook time: 2¼ hours | Serves 16

- 1 pound (454 g) ground beef
- ¼ cup finely chopped onion
- 1 (16-ounce / 454-g) package miniature hot dogs, drained
- 1 (12-ounce / 340-g) jar apricot preserves
- 1 cup barbecue sauce
- 1 (20-ounce / 567-g) can pineapple chunks, drained

1. In a large bowl, combine beef and onion, mixing lightly but thoroughly. Shape into 1-inch balls. In a large skillet over medium heat, cook meatballs in two batches until cooked through, turning occasionally. 2. Using a slotted spoon, transfer meatballs to a 3-quart crock pot. Add the hot dogs; stir in the preserves and barbecue sauce. Cook, covered, on high 2 to 3 hours or until heated through. 3. Stir in the pineapple; cook, covered, 15 to 20 minutes longer or until mixture is heated through.

Roasted Tomato and Mozzarella Bruschetta

Prep time: 15 minutes | Cook time: 5 hours | Serves 8

- ¼ cup extra-virgin olive oil
- 1 large red onion, coarsely chopped
- 2 teaspoons dried basil
- 1 teaspoon fresh rosemary leaves, finely chopped
- 4 cloves garlic, minced
- 3 (28- to 32-ounce / 794- to

- 907-g) cans whole plum tomatoes, drained
- 2 teaspoons salt
- ⅛ teaspoon red pepper flakes
- 8 ounces (227 g) fresh Mozzarella, cut into ½-inch dice

1. Lightly toasted baguette slices for serving 2. Combine all the ingredients except the Mozzarella and the baguette slices in the insert of a 5- to 7-quart crock pot. Cover and cook on high for 2 hours. Uncover the cooker and cook on low, stirring occasionally, for 3 hours, until the tomato liquid has almost evaporated. 3. Remove the tomato mixture to the bowl of a food processor and pulse on and off five times to chop the tomatoes and garlic. Transfer to a serving bowl to cool, then stir in the Mozzarella. 4. Serve with the toasted baguette slices.

Mini Hot Dogs

Prep time: 5 minutes | Cook time: 4 to 5 hours | Serves 20 to 30 as an appetizer

- 2 cups brown sugar
- 1 tablespoon Worcestershire sauce
- 1 (14-ounce / 397-g) bottle

- ketchup
- 2 or 3 pounds (907 g or 1.4 kg) mini-hot dogs

1. In crock pot, mix together brown sugar, 2. Worcestershire sauce, and ketchup. Stir in hot dogs. 3. Cover and cook on high 1 hour. Turn to low and cook 3 to 4 hours. 4. Serve from the cooker while turned to low.

Bacon-Pineapple Tater Tot Bake

Prep time: 15 minutes | Cook time: 4 hours | Serves 8

- 1 (32-ounce / 907-g) package frozen tater tots, thawed
- 8 ounces (227 g) Canadian bacon, chopped
- 1 cup frozen pepper strips, thawed and chopped
- 1 medium onion, finely chopped
- 1 (8-ounce / 227-g) can

- pineapple tidbits, drained
- 2 eggs
- 3 (5-ounce / 142-g) cans evaporated milk
- 1 (15-ounce / 425-g) can pizza sauce
- 1 cup shredded provolone cheese
- ½ cup grated Parmesan cheese (optional)

1. Place half of the Tater Tots in a greased 5-quart crock pot.

Layer with Canadian bacon, peppers, onion and pineapple. Top with remaining Tater Tots. In a large bowl, whisk eggs, milk and pizza sauce; pour over top. Sprinkle with provolone cheese. 2. Cook, covered, on low 4 to 5 hours or until heated through. If desired, sprinkle with Parmesan cheese; let stand, covered, 20 minutes.

Southwestern Chili con Queso

Prep time: 20 minutes | Cook time: 2 to 3 hours | Serves 8

- 1 (8-ounce / 227-g) package cream cheese, cut into cubes
- 2 tablespoons unsalted butter
- 1 medium sweet onion, such as Vidalia, finely chopped
- 4 chipotle chiles in adobo, minced
- 1 medium red bell pepper, seeded and finely chopped

- 1 medium yellow bell pepper, seeded and finely chopped
- 2 teaspoons ground cumin
- 2 cups finely shredded sharp Cheddar cheese
- 2 cups finely shredded Monterey Jack cheese
- Fresh vegetables for serving
- Tortilla chips for serving

1. Coat the insert of a 1½- to 3-quart crock pot with nonstick cooking spray. Turn the machine on low and add the cream cheese. Cover and let stand while preparing the other ingredients. 2. Melt the butter in a large sauté pan over medium-high heat. Add the onion, chipotles, bell peppers, and cumin and sauté until the bell peppers become softened, 4 to 5 minutes. Transfer the contents of the sauté pan into the crock pot insert and stir to blend with the cream cheese. 3. Fold in the Cheddar and Jack cheeses. Cover and cook on low for 2 to 3 hours. 4. Serve from the cooker set on warm with fresh vegetables and sturdy tortilla chips.

All American Snack

Prep time: 10 minutes | Cook time: 3 hours | Makes 3 quarts snack mix

- 3 cups thin pretzel sticks
- 4 cups Wheat Chex
- 4 cups Cheerios
- 1 (12-ounce / 340-g) can salted peanuts
- ¼ cup butter, melted

- 1 teaspoon garlic powder
- 1 teaspoon celery salt
- ½ teaspoon seasoned salt
- 2 tablespoons grated Parmesan cheese

1. Combine pretzels, cereal, and peanuts in large bowl. 2. Melt butter. Stir in garlic powder, celery salt, seasoned salt, and Parmesan cheese. Pour over pretzels and cereal. Toss until well mixed. 3. Pour into large crock pot. Cover. Cook on low 2½ hours, stirring every 30 minutes. Remove lid and cook another 30 minutes on low. 4. Serve warm or at room temperature. Store in tightly covered container.

Sweet 'n Sour Meatballs

Prep time: 10 minutes | Cook time: 2 to 4 hours | Serves 15 to 20

- 1 (12-ounce / 340-g) jar grape jelly
- 1 (12-ounce / 340-g) jar chili sauce
- 2 (1-pound / 454-g) bags prepared frozen meatballs, thawed

1. Combine jelly and sauce in crock pot. Stir well. 2. Add meatballs. Stir to coat. 3. Cover and heat on low 4 hours, or on high 2 hours. Keep crock pot on low while serving.

Mustard-Lovers' Party Dogs

Prep time: 15 minutes | Cook time: 1 to 2 hours | Serves 12

- 12 hot dogs, cut into bite-size pieces
- 1 cup grape jelly
- 1 cup prepared mustard

1. Place all ingredients in crock pot. Stir well. 2. Turn on high until mixture boils. Stir. 3. Turn to low and bring to the buffet table.

Hot Dill and Swiss Dip

Prep time: 10 minutes | Cook time: 2 to 3 hours | Serves 8

- 2 medium sweet onions, such as Vidalia, finely chopped
- 2 tablespoons finely chopped fresh dill
- 1½ cups mayonnaise
- 2 cups finely shredded Havarti with dill
- 2 cups finely shredded Swiss cheese

1. Coat the insert of a 1½- to 3-quart crock pot with nonstick cooking spray. Combine all the ingredients in a bowl and transfer to the crock pot. Cover and cook on low for 2 to 3 hours, until bubbling. 2. Serve from the cooker set on warm.

Barbecued Lil' Smokies

Prep time: 5 minutes | Cook time: 4 hours | Serves 48 to 60 as an appetizer

- 4 (16-ounce / 454-g) packages little smokies
- 1 (18-ounce / 510-g) bottle barbecue sauce

1. Mix ingredients together in crock pot. 2. Cover and cook on low for 4 hours.

Meaty Buffet Favorites

Prep time: 5 minutes | Cook time: 2 hours | Serves 24

- 1 cup tomato sauce
- 1 teaspoon Worcestershire sauce
- ½ teaspoon prepared
- mustard
- 2 tablespoons brown sugar
- 1 pound (454 g) prepared meatballs or mini-wieners

1. Mix first four ingredients in crock pot. 2. Add meatballs or mini-wieners. 3. Cover and cook on high for 2 hours. Turn to low and serve as an appetizer from the crock pot.

Buffalo Wing Dip

Prep time: 20 minutes | Cook time: 2 hours | Makes 6 cups

- 2 (8-ounce / 227-g) packages cream cheese, softened
- ½ cup ranch salad dressing
- ½ cup sour cream
- 5 tablespoons crumbled blue cheese
- 2 cups shredded cooked chicken
- ½ cup Buffalo wing sauce
- 2 cups shredded cheddar cheese, divided
- 1 green onion, sliced
- Tortilla chips

1. In a small bowl, combine the cream cheese, dressing, sour cream and blue cheese. Transfer to a 3-quart crock pot. Layer with chicken, wing sauce and 1 cup cheese. Cover and cook on low for 2 to 3 hours or until heated through. 2. Sprinkle with remaining cheese and onion. Serve with tortilla chips.

Creamy Cranberry Meatballs

Prep time: 15 minutes | Cook time: 2 to 6 hours | Serves 6

- 50 meatballs, about 1½ pounds (680 g)
- 1 cup brown gravy, from a jar, or made from a mix
- 1 cup whole-berry cranberry sauce
- 2 tablespoons heavy cream
- 2 teaspoons Dijon mustard

1. Put meatballs in crock pot. 2. Mix remaining ingredients in a bowl. Pour over meatballs. 3. Cover and cook on high 2 to 3 hours or on low 5 to 6 hours.

Chapter 9
Desserts

Cheesecake

Prep time: 25 minutes | Cook time: 2 hours | Serves 6

- Nonstick cooking spray
- Crust:
- ¾ cup graham cracker crumbs
- 2 tablespoons unsalted butter, melted
- 2 tablespoons sugar
- Filling:
- 16 ounces (454 g) cream cheese, softened
- ½ cup sugar
- 2 tablespoons all-purpose flour
- 2 teaspoon vanilla extract
- 2 large eggs, room temperature
- ½ cup plain yogurt or sour cream

1. Lightly coat a 6-inch springform pan with cooking spray; line bottom with parchment and lightly spray. Fill a 5- to 6-quart crock pot with ½ inch hot water. Set three 1-inch balls of foil in center of crock pot. Wrap crock pot lid tightly with a clean kitchen towel, gathering ends at top (to absorb condensation). Make the Crust: 2. Combine crumbs, butter, and sugar. Press mixture evenly on bottom and about 1 inch up sides of springform pan. Make the Filling: 3. In a food processor, pulse cream cheese, sugar, flour, and vanilla until smooth. Add eggs and process until combined. Add yogurt and process until smooth, scraping down sides of bowl. Pour filling into pan. Gently tap pan on work surface to remove air bubbles. 4. Set pan on aluminum balls in crock pot. Cover and cook on high until set and an instant-read thermometer inserted in center registers 155ºF (68ºC), 1½ to 2 hours (do not cook on low). Turn off crock pot and let cake rest, covered, 1 hour. 5. Carefully transfer pan to a wire rack to cool completely, then refrigerate until chilled, at least 4 hours and preferably overnight. Carefully remove outer ring from pan and transfer cake to a plate (remove parchment). Use a warm knife to cut into wedges, wiping blade after each cut.

Brownies with Nuts

Prep time: 15 minutes | Cook time: 3 hours | Makes 24 brownies

- Half a stick butter, melted
- 1 cup chopped nuts, divided
- 1 (23-ounce / 652-g) package brownie mix

1. Pour melted butter into a baking insert designed to fit into your crock pot. Swirl butter around to grease sides of insert. 2. Sprinkle butter with half the nuts. 3. In a bowl, mix brownies according to package directions. Spoon half the batter into the baking insert, trying to cover the nuts evenly. 4. Add remaining half of nuts. Spoon in remaining batter. 5. Place insert in crock pot. Cover insert with 8 paper towels. 6. Cover cooker. Cook on high 3 hours. Do not check or remove cover until last hour of cooking. Then insert toothpick into center of brownies. If it comes out clean, the brownies are finished. If it doesn't, continue cooking another 15 minutes. Check again. Repeat until pick comes out clean. 7. When finished cooking, uncover cooker and baking insert. Let brownies stand 5 minutes. 8. Invert insert onto serving plate. Cut brownies with a plastic knife (so the crumbs don't drag). Serve warm.

Blood Orange Upside-Down Cake

Prep time: 25 minutes | Cook time: 4 hours | Serves 6 to 8

- Orange Layer:
- 5 tablespoons unsalted butter, cut into small pieces, plus more for crock pot crock
- ¾ cup firmly packed dark brown sugar
- 3 tablespoons dark rum
- 2 pounds (907 g) blood oranges (about 6), sliced, peeled, with all of the bitter white pith removed
- ½ teaspoon ground cardamom
- Cake:
- ¾ cups cake flour
- ¾ teaspoons baking powder
- ½ teaspoon ground cinnamon
- ¼ teaspoon ground nutmeg
- ¼ teaspoon salt
- 4 tablespoons unsalted butter, at room temperature
- ⅔ cup granulated sugar
- 1 egg, at room temperature
- 1 egg yolk, at room temperature
- 2 tablespoons whole milk, at room temperature
- 2 cups vanilla ice cream, for serving (optional)

Make the Orange Layer: 1. Butter the inside of the crock pot crock, line completely with foil, and then butter the foil. 2. Sprinkle the butter, brown sugar, and rum over the foil on the bottom of the crock pot. Cover that with the orange slices in a slightly overlapping pattern, and sprinkle with the cardamom. Press the oranges into the sugar. Make the Cake: 3. Sift the flour, baking powder, cinnamon, nutmeg, and salt into a large bowl. Whisk gently to combine evenly. 4. In a medium bowl, slowly beat the butter and sugar with an electric mixer until just blended. Raise the speed to high and beat until light and fluffy, scraping down the sides of the bowl occasionally, about 10 minutes. 5. Beat the egg and then the egg yolk into the butter-sugar mixture, allowing each to be fully incorporated before adding the next. 6. While mixing slowly, add the flour mixture to the butter-sugar mixture in three parts, alternating with the milk in two parts, beginning and ending with the flour. Mix briefly at medium speed to make a smooth batter. 7. Pour the batter over the oranges in the crock pot and smooth with a spatula to even it out. 8. Lay a doubled length of paper towel from end to end over the top of the crock pot, to line the lid and create a tighter seal. 9. Cover the cake tightly with the lid and cook on high until the cake begins to brown slightly on the sides and springs back when touched in the middle, about 3½ hours. Turn off the crock pot and let the cake set, uncovered, about 20 minutes more. 10. Using the foil, lift the cake from the crock pot and set on the counter to cool, about 30 minutes more. Fold back the foil, and carefully invert the cake onto a platter so the caramelized oranges are visible on top. 11. Slice or spoon the cake into bowls, and serve with ice cream, if desired.

Bananas Foster Bread Pudding

Prep time: 15 minutes | Cook time: 3 hours | Serves 8

- ½ cup (1 stick) unsalted butter
- 2 cups firmly packed light brown sugar
- 4 medium bananas, cut into ½-inch rounds
- 8 large eggs
- 3 cups heavy cream
- ¼ cup dark rum
- 1 teaspoon ground cinnamon
- 1 tablespoon vanilla extract or vanilla bean paste
- 8 cups 1-inch cubes stale challah, egg bread, or Hawaiian sweet egg bread
- ¼ cup cinnamon sugar
- Whipped cream for serving

1. Coat the insert of a 5- to 7-quart crock pot with nonstick cooking spray or line the insert with a crock pot liner according to the manufacturer's directions. 2. Melt the butter in a large skillet over medium-high heat. Add 1 cup of the sugar and heat, stirring, until the sugar melts. Add the bananas and stir to coat. Remove the skillet from the heat and allow the bananas to cool slightly. 3. Whisk together the eggs, cream, remaining 1 cup sugar, rum, cinnamon, and vanilla in a large bowl. Add the bread to the custard and stir to blend, making sure to saturate the bread. Spoon half of the custard-soaked bread into the cooker and top with half the bananas. Repeat the layers, ending with the bananas. 4. Sprinkle the top with the cinnamon sugar. Cover and cook on high for about 3 hours, until puffed and an instant-read thermometer registers 185ºF (85ºC). Allow the pudding to cool for about 30 minutes. 5. Serve with whipped cream.

Sour Cream Amaretti Cheesecake

Prep time: 15 minutes | Cook time: 3 hours | Serves 6

- ¾ cup amaretti cookie crumbs (around 20 cookies, crushed)
- 2½ tablespoons unsalted butter, melted
- ½ teaspoon salt
- ¼ teaspoon ground cinnamon
- ⅓ cup granulated sugar,
- plus 1 tablespoon
- 12 ounces (340 g) cream cheese, at room temperature
- 1 tablespoon all-purpose flour
- 2 large eggs
- 1 teaspoon almond extract
- 1 cup sour cream

1. In a medium bowl, mix the cookie crumbs, melted butter, ¼ teaspoon of the salt, cinnamon, and 1 tablespoon sugar. Press the crumb mixture into a 6-inch springform pan, covering the bottom of pan and going about 1 inch up the side of the pan to form a crust. 2. With an electric mixer in a medium bowl, combine the cream cheese, flour, remaining ⅔ cup sugar, and remaining ¼ teaspoon salt. Beat at medium-high until smooth. 3. Scrape down the sides of bowl. Add the eggs and the almond extract. Beat until blended. 4. Add the sour cream and beat until smooth. 5. Pour the batter over the cookie crumb crust in the springform pan. 6. Fill the crock pot with ½ inch water and place the rack in the bottom, making sure the top of the rack is above the water. Set the springform pan with the cheesecake in it on the rack. Cover the crock pot with a triple layer of paper towels, and then cover with the lid. Cook on high for 2 hours without opening the crock pot even once. 7. Turn off the heat and let stand until cooker has cooled, again without opening lid, at least 1 additional hour. 8. Remove the cheesecake and chill for about 3 hours before serving in wedges.

Blueberry Crisp

Prep time: 10 minutes | Cook time: 3 to 4 hours | Serves 8

- 5 tablespoons coconut oil, melted, divided
- 4 cups blueberries
- ¾ cup plus 2 tablespoons granulated erythritol
- 1 cup ground pecans
- 1 teaspoon baking soda
- ½ teaspoon ground cinnamon
- 2 tablespoons coconut milk
- 1 egg

1. Lightly grease a 4-quart crock pot with 1 tablespoon of the coconut oil. 2. Add the blueberries and 2 tablespoons of erythritol to the insert. 3. In a large bowl, stir together the remaining ¾ cup of the erythritol, ground pecans, baking soda, and cinnamon until well mixed. 4. Add the coconut milk, egg, and remaining coconut oil, and stir until coarse crumbs form. 5. Top the contents in the insert with the pecan mixture. 6. Cover and cook on low for 3 to 4 hours. 7. Serve warm.

Piña Colada Bread Pudding

Prep time: 15 minutes | Cook time: 3 hours | Serves 6 to 8

- 8 cups torn stale Hawaiian sweet egg bread, challah, or croissants
- 2 cups ½-inch chunks fresh pineapple
- 1 cup chopped macadamia nuts
- 1½ cups shredded
- sweetened coconut
- 3 cups heavy cream
- 8 large eggs
- 1 tablespoon vanilla extract or bean paste
- ¼ cup dark rum
- 1½ cups sugar

1. Coat the insert of a 5- to 7-quart crock pot with nonstick cooking spray or line it with a crock pot liner according to the manufacturer's directions. 2. Put the bread in the crock pot insert, add the pineapple, nuts, and coconut, and toss to combine. Whisk together the cream, eggs, vanilla, rum, and sugar in a large mixing bowl until blended. Pour over the bread and push the bread down to submerge it. 3. Cover and cook on high for about 3 hours, until puffed and an instant-read thermometer inserted in the center registers 185ºF (85ºC). Uncover and allow to cool for 30 minutes. 4. Serve from the cooker set on warm.

Lemon Poppy Seed Upside-Down Cake

Prep time: 15 minutes | Cook time: 2 to 2½ hours | Serves 8 to 10

- 1 package lemon poppy seed bread mix
- 1 egg
- 8 ounces (227 g) light sour cream
- ½ cup water
- Sauce:
- 1 tablespoon butter
- ¾ cup water
- ½ cup sugar
- ¼ cup lemon juice

1. Combine first four ingredients until well moistened. Spread in lightly greased crock pot. 2. Combine sauce ingredients in small saucepan. Bring to boil. Pour boiling mixture over batter. 3. Cover. Cook on high 2 to 2½ hours. Edges will be slightly brown. Turn heat off and leave in cooker for 30 minutes with cover slightly ajar. 4. When cool enough to handle, hold a large plate over top of cooker, then invert. 5. Allow to cool before slicing.

Stewed Apricots

Prep time: 10 minutes | Cook time: 2 to 4 hours | Serves 6 to 8

- 1⅓ pounds (605 g) dried apricots, pitted
- 1 teaspoon ground cinnamon
- 1 cup granulated sugar
- 1 to 1¼ cups water
- ⅓ cup heavy cream
- 2 tablespoons toasted almond slivers

1. Turn the crock pot to high and add the apricots, cinnamon, sugar, and water. 2. Cover and cook on high for 2 hours, or on low for 4 hours. 3. Leave to cool in a large bowl, then chill in the refrigerator. 4. Just before you're ready to serve, whip the cream. Serve chilled in individual glasses, topped with whipped cream and nuts.

Sweet Rice and Almond Porridge

Prep time: 10 minutes | Cook time: 6 hours | Serves 6 to 8

- ⅓ cup basmati rice
- ⅓ cup almonds
- 4 cups whole milk, divided
- ¾ cup sugar
- Generous pinch saffron strands (optional)
- 6 green cardamom pods, seeds only, pounded to a fine powder
- Handful of crushed unsalted pistachios, for garnish

1. Wash the rice and soak it in water for 30 minutes. 2. In a blender, grind the rice and almonds with about ⅔ cup of the milk to a coarse paste. 3. Add the remaining milk and blend to a smooth paste. 4. Pour the mixture into your crock pot. Cover and cook on high for 4 hours. 5. Add the sugar, saffron (if using), and pounded cardamom seeds. Cover and cook on low for 2 more hours. 6. Transfer into individual ceramic dishes or a large clay or earthenware pot, and leave to cool for 4 to 5 hours. 7. Garnish with pistachios and serve chilled.

Coconut Jasmine Rice Pudding

Prep time: 15 minutes | Cook time: 2½ to 3 hours | Serves 8

- 2 cups whole milk
- 1 cup sugar
- 2 cups heavy cream
- 4 large eggs, beaten
- 1 teaspoon ground cinnamon
- 1½ cups Jasmine rice, rinsed with cold water and drained
- 2 cups shredded coconut, toasted
- Whipped cream, cinnamon sugar, or chopped mangoes and pineapple, for garnish

1. Coat the insert of a 5- to 7-quart crock pot with nonstick cooking spray. Heat the milk in a small saucepan until small bubbles form at the edges of the pan. Remove from the heat. Add the sugar and whisk until dissolved. Whisk together the sweetened milk, cream, eggs, and cinnamon in a mixing bowl. Stir in the rice. Transfer the mixture to the crock pot insert. 2. Cover and cook on low for 2½ to 3 hours, until the pudding is set. Remove the cover, stir in the coconut, and cook covered for an additional 30 minutes. Allow the pudding to cool in the insert, then transfer it to a bowl. Cover with plastic wrap and refrigerate until cold. 3. Scoop the pudding into bowls and garnish with whipped cream.

Almond Pear Crumble

Prep time: 10 minutes | Cook time: 2½ hours | Serves 8

- 1 cup firmly packed light brown sugar
- ¼ cup amaretto liqueur
- ¾ cup (1½ sticks) unsalted butter, melted
- 8 large firm pears, peeled, cored and coarsely chopped
- ½ cup granulated sugar
- ½ cup all-purpose flour
- ¾ teaspoon ground cinnamon
- ¼ teaspoon freshly grated nutmeg
- ⅔ cup sliced almonds
- Whipped cream for serving

1. Coat the insert of a 5- to 7-quart crock pot with nonstick cooking spray. Add the brown sugar, amaretto, and ½ cup of the butter to the crock pot insert and stir until blended. Add the pears and turn the pears to coat with the syrup. 2. Stir together the granulated sugar, flour, cinnamon, nutmeg, and almonds in a small bowl. Drizzle the remaining ¼ cup butter into the flour mixture and stir with a fork until the mixture begins to form crumbs. Sprinkle over the top of the pears. Cover and cook on high for 2½ hours, until a skewer inserted into the crumble comes out clean. Uncover and allow to cool for 30 minutes. 3. Serve the crumble warm with a dollop of whipped cream.

"Baked" Custard

Prep time: 10 minutes | Cook time: 2 to 3 hours | Serves 5 to 6

- 2 cups whole milk
- 3 eggs, slightly beaten
- ⅓ cup plus ½ teaspoon
- sugar, divided
- 1 teaspoon vanilla
- ¼ teaspoon cinnamon

1. Heat milk in a small uncovered saucepan until a skin forms on top. Remove from heat and let cool slightly. 2. Meanwhile, in a large mixing bowl combine eggs, ⅓ cup sugar, and vanilla. 3. Slowly stir cooled milk into egg-sugar mixture. 4. Pour into a greased 1-quart baking dish which will fit into your crock pot, or into a baking insert designed for your crock pot. 5. Mix cinnamon and ½ teaspoon reserved sugar in a small bowl. Sprinkle over custard mixture. 6. Cover baking dish or insert with foil. Set container on a metal rack or trivet in crock pot. Pour hot water around dish to a depth of 1 inch. 7. Cover cooker. Cook on high 2 to 3 hours, or until custard is set. (When blade of a knife inserted in center of custard comes out clean, custard is set.) 8. Serve warm from baking dish or insert.

Crunchy Candy Clusters

Prep time: 15 minutes | Cook time: 1 hour | Makes 6½ dozen

- 2 pounds (907 g) white candy coating, coarsely chopped
- 1½ cups peanut butter
- ½ teaspoon almond extract
- (optional)
- 4 cups Cap'n Crunch cereal
- 4 cups crisp rice cereal
- 4 cups miniature marshmallows

1. Place candy coating in a 5-quart crock pot. Cover and cook on high for 1 hour. Add peanut butter. Stir in extract if desired. 2. In a large bowl, combine the cereals and marshmallows. Stir in the peanut butter mixture until well coated. Drop by tablespoonfuls onto waxed paper. Let stand until set. Store at room temperature.

Peanut Butter Cake

Prep time: 10 minutes | Cook time: 2 to 3 hours | Serves 6

- 2 cups yellow cake mix
- ⅓ cup crunchy peanut
- butter
- ½ cup water

1. Combine all ingredients in electric mixer bowl. Beat with electric mixer about 2 minutes. 2. Pour batter into greased and floured baking pan insert, designed to fit inside your crock pot. 3. Place baking pan insert into crock pot. Cover with 8 paper towels. 4. Cover cooker. Cook on high 2 to 3 hours, or until toothpick inserted into center of cake comes out clean. About 30 minutes before the end of the cooking time, remove the cooker's lid, but keep the paper towels in place. 5. When cake is fully cooked, remove insert from crock pot. Turn insert upside-down on a serving plate and remove cake.

Cranberry Pudding

Prep time: 20 minutes | Cook time: 3 to 4 hours | Serves 8 to 10

- Pudding:
- 1⅓ cups flour
- ½ teaspoon salt
- 2 teaspoons baking soda
- ⅓ cup boiling water
- ½ cup dark molasses
- 2 cups whole cranberries
- ½ cup chopped nuts
- ½ cup water
- Butter Sauce:
- 1 cup confectioners sugar
- ½ cup heavy cream or evaporated milk
- ½ cup butter
- 1 teaspoon vanilla

1. Mix together flour and salt. 2. Dissolve soda in boiling water. Add to flour and salt. 3. Stir in molasses. Blend well. 4. Fold in cranberries and nuts. 5. Pour into well greased and floured bread or cake pan that will sit in your cooker. Cover with greased foil. 6. Pour ½ cup water into cooker. Place foil-covered pan in cooker. Cover with cooker lid and steam on high 3 to 4 hours, or until pudding tests done with a wooden pick. 7. Remove pan and uncover. Let stand 5 minutes, then unmold. 8. To make butter sauce, mix together all ingredients in saucepan. Cook, stirring over medium heat until sugar dissolves.

Peanut Butter Cheesecake

Prep time: 15 minutes | Cook time: 5 to 6 hours | Serves 10

- ¼ cup butter, melted, divided
- 1 cup ground almonds
- 2 tablespoons cocoa powder
- 1 cup granulated erythritol, divided
- 12 ounces (340 g) cream cheese, room temperature
- ½ cup natural peanut butter
- 2 eggs, room temperature
- 1 teaspoon pure vanilla extract

1. Lightly grease a 7-inch springform pan with 1 tablespoon butter. 2. In a small bowl, stir together the almonds, cocoa powder, and ¼ cup erythritol until blended. Add the remaining 3 tablespoons of the butter and stir until coarse crumbs form. 3. Press the crust mixture into the springform pan along the bottom and about 2 inches up the sides. 4. In a large bowl, using a handheld mixer, beat together the cream cheese and peanut butter until smooth. Beat in the remaining ¾ cup of the erythritol, eggs, and vanilla. 5. Spoon the batter into the springform pan and smooth out the top. 6. Place a wire rack in the insert of crock pot and place the springform pan on the wire rack. 7. Cover and cook on low for 5 to 6 hours, or until the cheesecake doesn't jiggle when shaken. 8. Cool completely before removing from pan. 9. Chill the cheesecake completely before serving, and store leftovers in the refrigerator.

Warm Gingerbread

Prep time: 10 minutes | Cook time: 3 hours | Serves 8

- 1 tablespoon coconut oil
- 2 cups almond flour
- ¾ cup granulated erythritol
- 2 tablespoons coconut flour
- 2 tablespoons ground ginger
- 2 teaspoons baking powder
- 2 teaspoons ground cinnamon
- ½ teaspoon ground nutmeg
- ¼ teaspoon ground cloves
- Pinch salt
- ¾ cup heavy (whipping) cream
- ½ cup butter, melted
- 4 eggs
- 1 teaspoon pure vanilla extract

1. Lightly grease the insert of the crock pot with coconut oil. 2. In a large bowl, stir together the almond flour, erythritol, coconut flour, ginger, baking powder, cinnamon, nutmeg, cloves, and salt. 3. In a medium bowl, whisk together the heavy cream, butter, eggs, and vanilla. 4. Add the wet ingredients to the dry ingredients and stir to combine. 5. Spoon the batter into the insert. 6. Cover and cook on low for 3 hours, or until a toothpick inserted in the center comes out clean. 7. Serve warm.

Five-Spice Asian Pears

Prep time: 10 minutes | Cook time: 2½ hours | Serves 8

- ½ cup (1 stick) unsalted butter, melted
- 1½ cups firmly packed light brown sugar
- ½ cup dry sherry
- 1 teaspoon five-spice powder
- 1 cup pear nectar
- 8 firm pears, peeled, halved, and cored

1. Mix together the butter, sugar, sherry, five-spice powder, and pear nectar in the insert of a 5- to 7-quart crock pot. Add the pears to the crock pot insert and turn to coat them with the liquid. Cover and cook on high for 2½ hours until tender. 2. Remove the pears with a slotted spoon to a serving bowl and spoon the liquid from the crock pot over the pears. Serve warm or chilled.

Apple Cobbler

Prep time: 20 minutes | Cook time: 4 hours | Serves 2

- Nonstick cooking spray
- 3 apples, peeled and sliced
- 1 tablespoon freshly squeezed lemon juice
- ½ cup dried cranberries
- ½ cup chopped walnuts
- ¼ cup granulated sugar,
- plus cup, divided
- ⅔ cup all-purpose flour
- ½ teaspoon baking powder
- 1 egg, beaten
- ⅔ cup milk
- 1 teaspoon vanilla

1. Spray the crock pot with the nonstick cooking spray. 2. Place the apples in the crock pot, sprinkle with the lemon juice, and toss. Add the cranberries and walnuts, sprinkle with ¼ cup of granulated sugar, and toss again. 3. In a medium bowl, stir the flour, the remaining ⅓ cup of granulated sugar, the baking powder, egg, milk, and vanilla until smooth. Spoon the mixture over the apples in the crock pot. 4. Cover and cook on low for 4 hours, or until the topping is set. 5. Serve warm with cream or ice cream.

Stuffed Spiced Apples

Prep time: 10 minutes | Cook time: 2 to 5 hours | Serves 4

- 4 medium-sized tart cooking apples (like Granny Smith or Braeburn)
- ⅓ cup finely chopped dried figs or raisins
- ½ cup finely chopped walnuts
- ¼ cup packed light brown sugar
- ½ teaspoon apple pie spice or cinnamon
- ¼ cup apple juice
- 1 tablespoon butter, cut into 4 pieces

1. Core the apples. Cut a strip of peel from the top of each apple. Place the apples upright in the crock pot. 2. In a small bowl, combine figs, walnuts, brown sugar, and apple pie spice. Spoon the mixture into the center of the apples, patting in with a knife or a narrow metal spatula. 3. Pour the apple juice around the apples in the crock pot. 4. Top each apple with a piece of butter. 5. Cover and cook on low for 4 to 5 hours or on high for 2 to 2½ hours until very tender. 6. Serve warm, with some of the cooking liquid spooned over the apples.

Mom's Old-Fashioned Rice Pudding

Prep time: 10 minutes | Cook time: 2½ to 3 hours | Serves 6 to 8

- 5 cups whole milk
- 2 cups heavy cream
- 1¼ cups sugar
- 1 teaspoon vanilla bean paste
- ½ teaspoon freshly grated
- nutmeg
- 1 cup Arborio or other medium-grain rice, rinsed several times with cold water and drained

1. Coat the insert of a 5- to 7-quart crock pot with nonstick cooking spray. Whisk together the milk, cream, sugar, vanilla bean paste, and nutmeg in a large bowl and pour into the crock pot insert. Add the rice and stir to combine. 2. Cover and cook on low for 2½ to 3 hours, until the pudding is soft and creamy and the rice is tender. Remove the cover, turn off the cooker, and allow to cool for 30 minutes. 3. Serve warm, at room temperature, or chilled.

Bananas Foster

Prep time: 10 minutes | Cook time: 1¼ hours | Serves 8

- Nonstick cooking oil spray
- 1 cup dark brown sugar
- ¼ cup butter
- ¼ cup dark rum
- ¼ cup banana liqueur
- ½ teaspoon ground

- cinnamon
- 4 ripe bananas, cut in half lengthwise, then halved crosswise
- 2 cups vanilla ice cream, for serving

1. Coat the interior of the crock pot crock with nonstick cooking oil spray. 2. Combine the brown sugar, butter, rum, and banana liqueur in the crock pot. 3. Cover and cook on low for 1 hour. Stir the sauce with a whisk until smooth. 4. Add the cinnamon and bananas to the sauce, and spoon the sauce over to coat. Cover and cook on low for 15 minutes. 5. Serve hot with a scoop of ice cream.

Tapioca

Prep time: 10 minutes | Cook time: 3½ hours | Serves 10 to 12

- 2 quarts whole milk
- 1¼ cups sugar
- 1 cup dry small pearl tapioca

- 4 eggs
- 1 teaspoon vanilla
- Whipped topping (optional)

1. Combine milk and sugar in crock pot, stirring until sugar is dissolved as well as possible. Stir in tapioca. 2. Cover and cook on high 3 hours. 3. In a small mixing bowl, beat eggs slightly. Beat in vanilla and about 1 cup hot milk from crock pot. When well mixed, stir into crock pot. 4. Cover and cook on high 20 more minutes. 5. Chill for several hours. Serve with whipped topping if you wish.

Brownie Chocolate Cake

Prep time: 10 minutes | Cook time: 3 hours | Serves 12

- ½ cup plus 1 tablespoon unsalted butter, melted, divided
- 1½ cups almond flour
- ¾ cup cocoa powder
- ¾ cup granulated erythritol
- 1 teaspoon baking powder

- ¼ teaspoon fine salt
- 1 cup heavy (whipping) cream
- 3 eggs, beaten
- 2 teaspoons pure vanilla extract
- 1 cup whipped cream

1. Generously grease the insert of the crock pot with 1 tablespoon of the melted butter. 2. In a large bowl, stir together the almond flour, cocoa powder, erythritol, baking powder, and salt. 3. In a medium bowl, whisk together the remaining ½ cup of the melted butter, heavy cream, eggs, and vanilla until well blended. 4. Whisk the wet ingredients into the dry ingredients

and spoon the batter into the insert. 5. Cover and cook on low for 3 hours, and then remove the insert from the crock pot and let the cake sit for 1 hour. 6. Serve warm with the whipped cream.

Apple-Pear Sauce

Prep time: 20 minutes | Cook time: 8 hours | Makes 8 cups

- Nonstick cooking spray
- 4 apples, peeled and sliced
- 3 firm pears, peeled and sliced
- ¼ cup apple cider
- ½ cup granulated sugar
- 2 tablespoons freshly

- squeezed lemon juice
- 1 teaspoon ground cinnamon
- 1 teaspoon ground nutmeg
- ⅛ teaspoon salt
- 1 teaspoon vanilla

1. Spray the crock pot with the nonstick cooking spray. 2. In the crock pot, combine the apples and pears, and stir. 3. Add the apple cider, sugar, lemon juice, cinnamon, nutmeg, and salt, and mix. 4. Cover and cook on low for 7 to 8 hours, or until the fruit is very soft. 5. Using a fork or potato masher, mash the mixture to the desired consistency. Stir in the vanilla and remove from the crock pot. 6. Serve immediately or cool and then refrigerate for up to 4 days or freeze.

Pots de Crème

Prep time: 10 minutes | Cook time: 1½ to 2 hours | Serves 6 to 8

- 8 to 10 cups boiling water
- ¾ cup whole milk
- ¾ cup heavy cream
- 1 cup chopped semisweet chocolate

- 4 large egg yolks
- ⅓ cup sugar
- Unsweetened whipped cream for serving

1. Place a crock pot insert rack on the bottom of a 5- to 7-quart crock pot and set out 6 (4-ounce / 113-g) ramekins. 2. Pour in enough of the boiling water to come halfway up the sides of the ramekins when they are eventually added to the cooker. Cover the cooker and set on high to keep the water hot. 3. Heat the milk and cream in a medium saucepan until small bubbles begin to form around the edges of the pan. Remove from the heat, add the chocolate, and stir until the chocolate is melted and the mixture is slightly cooled. 4. Whisk together the egg yolks and sugar in a mixing bowl, then whisk in the chocolate mixture. Strain the custard through a fine-mesh sieve into a large measuring cup. Pour the custard into the ramekins, cover each one with aluminum foil, and set on the rack in the crock pot insert. 5. Cover and cook on high for 1½ to 2 hours, until set. They may be a bit jiggly in the middle but they will firm as they cool. Remove the foil, allow the custards to cool to room temperature, and refrigerate until chilled. 6. Serve the pots de crème with a dollop of whipped cream on top.

Chocolate-Chile Cheesecake

Prep time: 15 minutes | Cook time: 2½ hours | Serves 8 to 10

- Crust:
- 3 cups chocolate digestive biscuits (or chocolate graham crackers, or any plain chocolate cookies), crushed
- 1 tablespoon unsweetened cocoa powder
- ⅔ cup unsalted butter, melted
- Filling:
- 1 pound (454 g) cream cheese
- ⅔ cup sour cream
- 3 large eggs, plus 3 egg yolks
- ¾ cup sugar
- 5 to 6 ounces (142 to 170 g) dark chocolate (you can use chili chocolate)
- ½ tablespoon unsweetened cocoa powder mixed with 1 tablespoon hot water
- 3 to 4 dried chiles, very finely crushed

Make the Crust: 1. Place a rack in the bottom of the crock pot, or scrunch up foil to create a zigzag across the bottom of the cooker so a cake pan can sit on top of it. Add about 1 cup of hot water. 2. Grease a 7-inch springform pan. 3. Mix the crushed biscuits, cocoa, and melted butter, and press the mixture into the bottom of the springform pan. Even the layer out and put it into the freezer for about 10 minutes. Make the Filling: 4. In a large bowl, beat the cream cheese to soften. Then add the sour cream, followed by the eggs and egg yolks. Beat in the sugar until it's all mixed together. 5. Simmer some water in a pan and place the chocolate into a glass bowl that will sit over the pan but not touch the water. Melt the chocolate gently and set aside. (You can also put the chocolate in a bowl and melt it in the microwave for 1 minute on high. Stir to ensure it has melted through.) 6. In a smaller bowl, combine the melted chocolate and the cocoa-and-water mixture, and then add the crushed chiles and mix well. Add the chile mixture to the cream mixture and mix completely so it's smooth. 7. Take the crust out of the freezer, and line the outside of the springform with foil. Pour the chocolate filling into the pan. 8. Place it gently onto the rack or foil in the crock pot, so it's not touching the sides. 9. Switch the crock pot to high and put a kitchen towel over the top of the cooker. Place the lid on top of the towel and cook on high for 2½ hours. 10. Turn the cooker off, don't open it, and leave the cake to sit for another hour inside the cooker. 11. After an hour, remove the pan from the crock pot, take the foil off, and allow it to cool completely before refrigerating overnight. 12. To serve, let the cake stand at room temperature for about 20 minutes before removing it from the pan. Serve with a big dollop of whipped cream and enjoy!

Strawberry Rhubarb Crumble

Prep time: 10 minutes | Cook time: 2½ hours | Serves 8

- 4 cups strawberries, hulled and cut into quarters
- 4 stalks bright red rhubarb, cut into ½-inch slices
- 1½ cups granulated sugar
- 1 teaspoon ground cinnamon
- Grated zest of 1 orange
- 1 tablespoon cornstarch
- ⅔ cup old-fashioned rolled oats
- ¾ cup firmly packed light brown sugar
- ½ cup finely chopped white chocolate
- 1 cup all-purpose flour
- ½ cup (1 stick) unsalted butter, chilled and cut into ½-inch pieces
- Vanilla ice cream for serving

1. Coat the insert of a 5- to 7-quart crock pot with nonstick cooking spray. Stir the berries, rhubarb, granulated sugar, cinnamon, zest, and cornstarch together in the insert. Set aside while making the crumble. 2. Stir together the oats, brown sugar, chocolate, and flour in a mixing bowl. Add the butter and cut the butter into the dry ingredients, using a blending fork or pastry blender, until the mixture forms coarse crumbs about the size of peas. 3. Sprinkle the crumble over the fruit. Cover and cook on low for 2½ hours, until the crumble is set and the fruit is bubbling. Uncover the crock pot and allow to cool for 30 minutes. 4. Serve warm with vanilla ice cream.

Pumpkin-Ginger Pudding

Prep time: 5 minutes | Cook time: 3 to 4 hours | Serves 8

- 1 tablespoon coconut oil
- 2 cups pumpkin purée
- 1½ cups coconut milk
- 2 eggs
- ½ cup almond flour
- 1 ounce (28 g) protein powder
- 1 tablespoon grated fresh ginger
- ¾ teaspoon liquid stevia
- Pinch ground cloves
- 1 cup whipped coconut cream

1. Lightly grease the insert of the crock pot with coconut oil. 2. In a large bowl, stir together pumpkin, coconut milk, eggs, almond flour, protein powder, ginger, liquid stevia, and cloves. 3. Transfer the mixture to the insert. 4. Cover and cook on low 3 to 4 hours. 5. Serve warm with whipped coconut cream.

Chapter 10

Pizzas, Wraps, and Sandwiches

Beach Boy's Pot Roast

Prep time: 10 minutes | Cook time: 8 to 12 hours | Makes 6 to 8 sandwiches

- 1 (3- to 4-pound / 1.4- to 1.8-kg) chuck or top round roast
- 8 to 12 slivers of garlic
- 1 (32-ounce / 907-g) jar
- pepperoncini peppers, undrained
- 6 to 8 large hoagie rolls
- 12 to 16 slices of your favorite cheese

1. Cut slits into roast with a sharp knife and insert garlic slivers. 2. Place beef in crock pot. Spoon peppers and all of their juice over top. 3. Cover and cook on low 8 to 12 hours, or until meat is tender but not dry. 4. Remove meat from cooker and allow to cool. Then use 2 forks to shred the beef. 5. Spread on hoagie rolls and top with cheese.

Herby Beef Sandwiches

Prep time: 5 minutes | Cook time: 7 to 8 hours | Makes 10 to 12 sandwiches

- 1 (3- to 4-pound / 1.4- to 1.8-kg) boneless beef chuck roast
- 3 tablespoons fresh basil, or 1 tablespoon dried basil
- 3 tablespoons fresh
- oregano, or 1 tablespoon dried oregano
- 1½ cups water
- 1 package dry onion soup mix
- 10 to 12 Italian rolls

1. Place roast in crock pot. 2. Combine basil, oregano, and water. Pour over roast. 3. Sprinkle with onion soup mix. 4. Cover. Cook on low 7 to 8 hours. Shred meat with fork. 5. Serve on Italian rolls.

Mexican Shredded Beef Wraps

Prep time: 20 minutes | Cook time: 6 hours | Serves 6

- 1 small onion, finely chopped
- 1 jalapeno pepper, seeded and minced
- 3 garlic cloves, minced
- 1 (2- to 3-pound / 907-g to 1.4-kg) boneless beef chuck roast
- ½ teaspoon salt
- ½ teaspoon pepper
- 1 (8-ounce / 227-g) can
- tomato sauce
- ¼ cup lime juice
- 1 tablespoon chili powder
- 1 teaspoon ground cumin
- ¼ teaspoon cayenne pepper
- 6 flour or whole wheat tortillas
- Optional toppings: torn romaine, chopped tomatoes and sliced avocado

1. Place onion, jalapeno and garlic in a 4-quart crock pot. Sprinkle roast with salt and pepper; place over vegetables. In a small bowl, mix tomato sauce, lime juice, chili powder, cumin and cayenne; pour over roast. 2. Cook, covered, on low 6 to 8 hours or until meat is tender. Remove roast; cool slightly.

Shred meat with two forks; return to crock pot. Serve beef on tortillas with toppings of your choice.

Cuban-Style Pork Sandwiches

Prep time: 20 minutes | Cook time: 6 hours | Serves 10

- 1 large onion, cut into wedges
- ¾ cup reduced-sodium chicken broth
- 1 cup minced fresh parsley
- 7 garlic cloves, minced and divided
- 2 tablespoons cider vinegar
- 1 tablespoon plus 1½ teaspoons lemon juice, divided
- 2 teaspoons ground cumin
- 1 teaspoon ground mustard
- 1 teaspoon dried oregano
- ½ teaspoon salt
- ½ teaspoon pepper
- 1 (3- to 4-pound / 1.4- to 1.8-kg) boneless pork shoulder butt roast
- 1¼ cups fat-free mayonnaise
- 2 tablespoons Dijon mustard
- 10 whole wheat hamburger buns, split
- 1¼ cups shredded reduced-fat Swiss cheese
- 1 medium onion, thinly sliced an separated into rings
- 2 whole dill pickles, sliced

1. Place onion wedges and broth in a 5-quart crock pot. In a small bowl, combine the parsley, 5 garlic cloves, vinegar, 1 tablespoon lemon juice, cumin, mustard, oregano, salt and pepper; rub over pork. Add to crock pot. Cover and cook on low for 6 to 8 hours or until meat is tender. 2. Remove meat; let stand for 10 minutes before slicing. In another small bowl, combine the mayonnaise, mustard and remaining garlic and lemon juice; spread over buns. Layer bun bottoms with pork, cheese, sliced onion and pickles; replace tops. 3. Cook on a panini maker or indoor grill for 2 to 3 minutes or until buns brown and cheese melts.

Zesty French Sandwiches

Prep time: 5 minutes | Cook time: 8 hours | Makes 6 to 8 sandwiches

- 1 (4-pound / 1.8-kg) beef roast
- 1 (10½-ounce / 298-g) can beef broth
- 1 (10½-ounce / 298-g) can condensed French onion
- soup
- 1 (12-ounce / 340-g) bottle of beer
- 6 to 8 French rolls or baguettes

1. Pat roast dry and place in crock pot. 2. In a mixing bowl, combine beef broth, onion soup, and beer. Pour over meat. 3. Cover and cook on low 8 hours, or until meat is tender but not dry. 4. Split rolls or baguettes. Warm in the oven or microwave until heated through. 5. Remove meat from cooker and allow to rest for 10 minutes. Then shred with two forks, or cut on the diagonal into thin slices, and place in rolls. Serve.

Barbecue Sauce and Hamburgers

Prep time: 25 minutes | Cook time: 5 to 6 hours | Makes 6 sandwiches

- 1 (14¾-ounce / 418-g) can beef gravy
- ½ cup ketchup
- ½ cup chili sauce
- 1 tablespoon
- Worcestershire sauce
- 1 tablespoon prepared mustard
- 6 grilled hamburger patties
- 6 slices cheese (optional)

1. Combine all ingredients except hamburger patties and cheese slices in crock pot. 2. Add hamburger patties. 3. Cover. Cook on low 5 to 6 hours. 4. Serve in buns, each topped with a slice of cheese if you like.

Beef and Veggie Sloppy Joes

Prep time: 35 minutes | Cook time: 5 hours | Serves 12

- 4 medium carrots, shredded (about 3½ cups)
- 1 medium yellow summer squash, shredded (about 2 cups)
- 1 medium zucchini, shredded (about 2 cups)
- 1 medium sweet red pepper, finely chopped
- 2 medium tomatoes, seeded and chopped
- 1 small red onion, finely chopped
- ½ cup ketchup
- 3 tablespoons minced fresh basil or 3 teaspoons dried basil
- 3 tablespoons molasses
- 2 tablespoons cider vinegar
- 2 garlic cloves, minced
- ½ teaspoon salt
- ½ teaspoon pepper
- 2 pounds (907 g) lean ground beef (90% lean)
- 12 whole wheat hamburger buns, split

1. In a 5- or 6-quart crock pot, combine the first 13 ingredients. In a large skillet, cook beef over medium heat 8 to 10 minutes or until no longer pink, breaking into crumbles. Drain; transfer beef to crock pot. Stir to combine. 2. Cook, covered, on low 5 to 6 hours or until heated through and vegetables are tender. Using a slotted spoon, serve beef mixture on buns.

Middle-Eastern Sandwiches (for a crowd)

Prep time: 50 minutes | Cook time: 6 to 8 hours | Makes 10 to 16 sandwiches

- 4 pounds (1.8 kg) boneless beef or venison, cut in ½-inch cubes
- 4 tablespoons cooking oil
- 2 cups chopped onions
- 2 garlic cloves, minced
- 1 cup dry red wine
- 1 (6-ounce / 170-g) can tomato paste
- 1 teaspoon dried oregano
- 1 teaspoon dried basil
- ½ teaspoon dried rosemary
- 2 teaspoons salt
- Dash of pepper
- ¼ cup cold water
- ¼ cup cornstarch
- Pita pocket breads
- 2 cups shredded lettuce

- 1 large tomato, seeded and diced
- 1 large cucumber, seeded
- and diced
- 8 ounces (227 g) plain yogurt

1. Brown meat, 1 pound (454 g) at a time, in skillet in 1 tablespoon oil. Reserve drippings and transfer meat to crock pot. 2. Sauté onion and garlic in drippings until tender. Add to meat. 3. Add wine, tomato paste, oregano, basil, rosemary, salt, and pepper. 4. Cover. Cook on low 6 to 8 hours. 5. Turn cooker to high. Combine cornstarch and water in small bowl until smooth. Stir into meat mixture. Cook until bubbly and thickened, stirring occasionally. 6. Split pita breads to make pockets. Fill each with meat mixture, lettuce, tomato, cucumber, and yogurt. 7. Serve.

Tangy Barbecue Sandwiches

Prep time: 20 minutes | Cook time: 7 to 9 hours | Makes 14 to 18 sandwiches

- 3 cups chopped celery
- 1 cup chopped onions
- 1 cup ketchup
- 1 cup barbecue sauce
- 1 cup water
- 2 tablespoons vinegar
- 2 tablespoons Worcestershire sauce
- 2 tablespoons brown sugar
- 1 teaspoon chili powder
- 1 teaspoon salt
- ½ teaspoon pepper
- ½ teaspoon garlic powder
- 1 (3- to 4-pound / 1.4- to 1.8-kg) boneless chuck roast
- 14 to 18 hamburger buns

1. Combine all ingredients except roast and buns in crock pot. When well mixed, add roast. 2. Cover. Cook on high 6 to 7 hours. 3. Remove roast. Cool and shred meat. Return to sauce. Heat well. 4. Serve on buns.

Barbecued Beef Sandwiches

Prep time: 10 minutes | Cook time: 10 to 12 hours | Makes 18 to 20 sandwiches

- 1 (3½- to 4-pound / 1.6- to 1.8-kg) beef round steak, cubed
- 1 cup finely chopped onions
- ½ cup firmly packed brown sugar
- 1 tablespoon chili powder
- ½ cup ketchup
- ⅓ cup cider vinegar
- 1 (12-ounce / 340-g) can beer
- 1 (6-ounce / 170-g) can tomato paste
- Buns

1. Combine all ingredients except buns in crock pot. 2. Cover. Cook on low 10 to 12 hours. 3. Remove beef from sauce with slotted spoon. 4. Place in large bowl. Shred with 2 forks. Add 2 cups sauce from crock pot to shredded beef. Mix well. 5. Pile into buns and serve immediately.

Appendix 1

Measurement Conversion Chart

VOLUME EQUIVALENTS(DRY)

US STANDARD	METRIC (APPROXIMATE)
1/8 teaspoon	0.5 mL
1/4 teaspoon	1 mL
1/2 teaspoon	2 mL
3/4 teaspoon	4 mL
1 teaspoon	5 mL
1 tablespoon	15 mL
1/4 cup	59 mL
1/2 cup	118 mL
3/4 cup	177 mL
1 cup	235 mL
2 cups	475 mL
3 cups	700 mL
4 cups	1 L

VOLUME EQUIVALENTS(LIQUID)

US STANDARD	US STANDARD (OUNCES)	METRIC (APPROXIMATE)
2 tablespoons	1 fl.oz.	30 mL
1/4 cup	2 fl.oz.	60 mL
1/2 cup	4 fl.oz.	120 mL
1 cup	8 fl.oz.	240 mL
1 1/2 cup	12 fl.oz.	355 mL
2 cups or 1 pint	16 fl.oz.	475 mL
4 cups or 1 quart	32 fl.oz.	1 L
1 gallon	128 fl.oz.	4 L

TEMPERATURES EQUIVALENTS

FAHRENHEIT(F)	CELSIUS(C) (APPROXIMATE)
225 °F	107 °C
250 °F	120 °C
275 °F	135 °C
300 °F	150 °C
325 °F	160 °C
350 °F	180 °C
375 °F	190 °C
400 °F	205 °C
425 °F	220 °C
450 °F	235 °C
475 °F	245 °C
500 °F	260 °C

WEIGHT EQUIVALENTS

US STANDARD	METRIC (APPROXIMATE)
1 ounce	28 g
2 ounces	57 g
5 ounces	142 g
10 ounces	284 g
15 ounces	425 g
16 ounces (1 pound)	455 g
1.5 pounds	680 g
2 pounds	907 g

Appendix 2
Index

Made in United States
Orlando, FL
21 November 2024

54261061R00050